P9-DWK-255

TIMELESS LUXURY
Ninety Years of the Phantom

© REGAL PRESS 2015

PRESIDENT'S WELCOME

Greetings! We all enjoy sharing stories with our friends and celebrating anniversaries, and I have some of both for you.

The Rolls-Royce Owners' Club (RROC) is an organization dedicated to Bentley and Rolls-Royce automobiles. It started life as an owners' organization but today the only prerequisite for membership is enthusiasm for the marques. This enlightened and open policy has strengthened the club, which continues to attract enthusiasts from all over the world, who are interested in not only the cars but also the history and technology, as well as lifestyle and cultural aspects, associated with them.

The formation of the RROC was well underway by the spring of 1950. The club's first official meeting took place on May 12, 1951. This makes the RROC the oldest organization dedicated to both marques. At the time the club started, the latest models coming out of the factory in Crewe were the Bentley Mark VI and the Rolls-Royce Silver Wraith, Silver Dawn, and Phantom IV—the latter in the main available only to royalty or heads of state. The collector car movement was young in 1951 and the early members formed a club so as to help each other keep their cars running and enjoy the camaraderie they expected to find in organizing meets.

In 2015, the RROC celebrates its 64th anniversary, but it also celebrates the 90th anniversary of the Rolls-Royce New Phantom, the 60th anniversary of the Rolls-Royce Silver Cloud and Bentley S1, and the 50th anniversary of the Rolls-Royce Silver Shadow and Bentley T. The celebration of these anniversaries will be at its height during the RROC's signature event: the Annual Meet.

This week-long gathering is packed with activities, such as seminars, tours, and workshops. A grand feature is always the quantity and variety of automobiles that come to the meet. An even grander aspect is the role it plays in bringing members together from all corners of the country and the world.

In the pages that follow you will take a journey through a sampling of the rich history of the marques and some of what the RROC is all about, extending into areas of art, culture, luxury, and travel that resonate with the interests of our readers—a world of people, places, and things.

I wish to thank all the contributors to this book and all those whose efforts have made its production possible. Whether you're a member of the RROC or came across this book by some other means, I hope you will enjoy it and learn from it. Most every entry ends with a website to encourage further inquiry, starting with this one for the club itself: www.rroc.org.

Best wishes and happy motoring!

Rubén Verdés
President, Rolls-Royce Owners' Club

CONTENTS

Chapter 1
DRIVING EXCELLENCE

THE ART OF THE PHANTOM

The New Phantom body designs offered by US coachwork
company Brewster in 1925 were works of exquisite artistry,
as the accompanying catalog serves to illustrate

Above: "Piccadilly. The Clubman's Roadster. A model for four passengers. The rear seat is well designed and very comfortable. A convenient compartment in the body holds four golf bags"

ADVANCE SKETCHES
OF NEW COACHWORK
ROLLS-ROYCE

Founded in 1810, the American coachbuilder Brewster & Company of Long Island City, New York started bodying automobiles as early as 1896 on a variety of domestic and foreign chassis, beginning with the most desirable French car of the day, the Delauney-Belleville, which Brewster began importing in 1905.

The company's reputation for excellent work on this and other luxury chassis brought it to the attention of Rolls-Royce, which appointed Brewster as one of its US sales agents in 1914 and, after opening a US manufacturing facility, a supplier of bodies for such cars. When Brewster's position in the marketplace weakened, an amicable meeting of executives of both firms resulted in Rolls-Royce of America acquiring Brewster outright in 1929—and all should have been well.

Things didn't turn out that way, however. The Great Depression didn't help, but fundamentally different approaches to selling automobiles had, almost from the outset, caused friction among the staffs of the merged firms. By the time Rolls-Royce of America turned off the lights in 1931, William Brewster was a disillusioned man, even though he remained on friendly terms with his Rolls-Royce counterpart, Henry J. Fuller.

Twice in its history, Brewster produced complete cars of its own manufacture—once before and once after the relationship with Rolls-Royce. But what had once been opulent and expensive cars for a veritable who's who of high society became ever cheaper and less distinctive, and by 1937 Brewster was forced to close down.

Some of the more than two dozen bodies Brewster offered on the Rolls-Royce chassis were, and have remained, among the more desirable coachwork of the marque. The following pages show the beautifully illustrated 1925 catalog of New Phantom models, entitled *Advance Sketches of New Coachwork*.

ADVANCE SKETCHES OF ROLLS-ROYCE COACHWORK

THE most recent developments in de luxe body architecture and construction are herein presented in advance form. All are mounted on one type of chassis — the celebrated mechanism so long esteemed for its many features of great excellence. These models have left-side steering, specially designed by Mr. Royce for American driving conditions.

A PORTFOLIO OF COACHWORK WITH COLOR ILLUSTRATIONS AND EMBODYING THE AUTHORITATIVE POINTS OF INTEREST IN CORRECT COACHWORK TECHNIQUE WILL BE AVAILABLE SOON AND FURNISHED ON REQUEST

Reprinted 1974 by the Rolls Royce Owners Club of America

Copyright, 1925, by Rolls-Royce of America, Inc

PALL MALL

A FOUR-PASSENGER Phæton model, interpreting most attractively the smart open body of moderate size, intended principally for owner-driving

OXFORD

THIS design most admirably expresses the idea of exceptional comfort and spaciousness in a seven-passenger open model

TILBURY

DESIGNED particularly for the man or woman who prefers to drive. The solid rear quarters give privacy. There is no division between driving seat and rear compartment

PICKWICK

A SIX-PASSENGER model of special design, appropriate for either owner or chauffeur to drive. It has a division back of the front seat

———

BERWICK

EXACTLY like the Pickwick in appearance and arrangement, except that it does not have the partition back of the driver's seat

SUDBURY

ANOTHER smart model for the owner-driver. It resembles the Tilbury, but the rear quarter windows give more vision when this feature is preferred

BUCKINGHAM

THE long graceful body is the most characteristic feature of this design, yielding abundant room. The vertical windshield is supported on small pillars, giving clear vision

CANTERBURY

A SEVEN-PASSENGER design of particular interest on account of the clear vision afforded by the large specially designed windows

SALAMANCA
(COLLAPSIBLE)

A DEVELOPMENT of the distinctive Cabriolet design originally created for Rolls-Royce by the Count of Salamanca. The body is built collapsible, so that the rear portion can be folded down when required

MAYFAIR

A FORMAL Town Car of the full Cabriolet type, authoritative in its stylistic treatment of line and detail. It accommodates five persons in the body proper

SALAMANCA
(NON-COLLAPSIBLE)

THIS model is exactly the same in appearance and details as the Salamanca Collapsible Cabriolet, only the body is fixed and not convertible into an open car

THE EX FACTOR

*The emergence of the New Phantom 90 years ago was accompanied
by a series of experimental models, culminating in the production of
a unique motor car with a singular story*

A Rolls-Royce one-of-a-kind, the 17EX was the last in a series of experimental models developed in the latter part of the 1920s at the personal request of Henry Royce to explore the performance potential of the Phantom I chassis. In November 1925, Royce had expressed his disappointment that the recently introduced Phantom, with its overhead valve power unit, did not represent an improvement in terms of performance over the sidevalve Silver Ghost that it had replaced. Tests were carried out with chassis 10EX, fitted with a specially tuned engine and open sports tourer bodywork by Barker, but initially it proved only marginally faster than the standard model.

The project had been initiated with the full blessing of Rolls-Royce's commercial genius, managing director Claude Johnson, hence its in-house title "the CJ sports car." But Johnson died unexpectedly in 1926 and was succeeded by his more cautious brother Basil, who worried that the program might produce a "rough and noisy car, typical of the sports car of the day."

Smooth and silent

To reassure him, Henry Royce—who after all had initiated the project—wrote: "The object of preparing this chassis is that, if speed merchants in the form of English peers or Indian Rajahs or others doubt the capacity of the Rolls-Royce Phantom I, this specimen, which we should be able to repeat, can be tried by them … We have no thought of making a freak machine or to depart from the smooth and silent model, but we do think that the owners of the smooth and silent models within their large bodies capable of 80 mph will be pleased to know that the same chassis and engine, when fitted to a touring car, will be capable of 95–100 mph."

It was a line of thought that would ultimately lead to the Derby Bentley "silent sports car" of the 1930s, but in this early stage of Royce's quest to produce a car with "a bit of fizz," there was the problem that 10EX was not producing the hoped-for level of performance.

In the immortal words of Ettore Bugatti, of whose work Royce, as a former owner of a Type 13 Bugatti, was fully aware, "weight was the enemy."

Demands for greater levels of comfort and enhanced specifications were offsetting the extra power developed by the new engine. Rolls-Royce designer Ivan Evernden, who worked in the little studio established near Royce's summer home at West Wittering in Sussex, recalled that: "Since 1911, cars, besides becoming materially bigger, had become disproportionately heavier. This fact, together with tires of large section and lower pressure, caused an increase in road rolling resistance. Even more important was the fact that the wind drag of the car had increased enormously due chiefly to the increase in the frontal projected area. The front fenders had grown to envelop the wheels, headlamps had risen to add to the frontal area of the taller radiator and the higher hood and scuttle. Also, there was little improvement in the aerodynamic form."

Extra power was not the answer: opening the exhaust cutout—illegal, anyway, in Great Britain—added an extra 11 hp, but only increased speed by 2 mph. So W. A. Robotham, assistant to Ernest Hives, head of the Experimental

Previous pages: 17EX in its full
present-day glory

Above: Designer Ivan Evernden
(background) and Henry Royce

Opposite: The car's experimental
predecessor, 10EX

"EVERNDEN OBTAINED A SLAB OF BALSA WOOD AND MADE A ONE-EIGHTH SCALE MODEL OF THE REQUIRED MODIFICATIONS"

Department, carried out a series of tests on the Brooklands race track, progressively removing fenders, sidemount spare wheels, headlamps, and windshield. The results were remarkable: removing the fenders alone gave an increase of 6.4 mph in maximum speed, while the windshield, sidemount, and under-hood ventilation were found to create a total of 11.4 mph worth of drag.

New body design

Ivan Evernden was given the task of developing a new type of body design that would incorporate the results of these tests to produce an enhanced level of performance. He would spend almost a year developing a more efficient body shape. A major obstacle, he quickly discovered, was the entrenched attitude of many of the companies who erected bodies on Rolls-Royce chassis: "The classic coachbuilder of the day, a craftsman whose ancestors had built carriages for the landed aristocracy … was an artist, but certainly not a scientist or an engineer. His methods of body construction were still those evolved in the days of the horsedrawn carriage and were totally inadequate to cope with the stresses set up in the motorcar capable of almost five times the speed. To cope with body cracking, more and more wrought iron was introduced into the structure without an adequate reward in an increase of strength."

A further problem for Evernden was that the Rolls-Royce management was reluctant to spend much money on his researches as the company did not build its own bodywork and felt that the coachbuilders should be funding at least part of the project.

He had the happy idea that an acceptable result could be achieved at minimum cost by reworking the Barker tourer bodywork on 10EX. Finding it difficult to explain the desired shape to the coachbuilders, Evernden obtained a slab of balsa wood and some sheet aluminum from Hives and, working in Royce's own workshop beside his garage at West Wittering, he made a one-eighth scale model of the required modifications. Barker agreed to carry out the work for £300, and cut off the existing body behind the front seats to graft on the new aerodynamic rear end designed by Evernden; new fenders and windshield were also fitted, and the front seats and steering wheel lowered by four inches. Very much in the spirit of the contemporary Art Deco movement, the revised body tapered both horizontally and vertically at the rear.

Evernden collected 10EX from Barker on April 9 and it was then delivered to Derby by works test driver George Ratcliffe for work to be carried out on the chassis.

Preliminary road testing revealed that the high-speed performance of 10EX had been

Right and opposite: 10EX's open sports
tourer bodywork, including aerodynamic
rear, on view at two UK meets

"materially improved" by the modifications; it was found to be both faster and to hold the road better. Finally, the car was driven down to Royce's summer home in Sussex at the end of April for his approval.

Always the perfectionist, he called for improvements to be made to the steering and suspension; these improvements would find their way on to production Phantoms.

After a further spell at Derby, 10EX was sent to the eastcoast town of Frinton where Basil Johnson was on holiday, the staid reputation of this upper-crust seaside resort town doubtless reflecting Johnson's conservative nature. Inevitably, he had reservations about the car's adventurous styling: "We realize that this car is only an experiment, and we are hopeful of being able to improve its appearance."

But further tests at Brooklands against a standard Rolls-Royce touring car proved the rightness of Evernden's design; with the cut-out open, the "CJ sports car" recorded a top speed of 89.11 mph against the 78.26 mph of the standard car, and removing its flared front fenders only added an extra three miles an hour.

These impressive figures were achieved with the standard final drive ratio, and the engine was peaking well before the top speed was reached; a taller final drive gearing was called for. But the improvised nature of the modifications to 10EX meant that this could only be achieved with a substantial weight reduction—the car tipped the scales at a substantial 2.35 tons unladen —to maintain the car's rate of acceleration.

Nevertheless, tests with a 17-tooth pinion, instead of the standard 16-tooth gear, produced an extra 1.4 mph in adverse weather conditions, with the promise of more on a calmer day. The decision was taken to go ahead with the production of three very special Phantoms based on the design of 10EX, but with lighter bodies to justify the use of the taller gearing. Their chassis numbers were 15EX, 16EX and 17EX (though the chassis card of 17EX specifies the 16 x 52 gear set, perhaps in view of the terrain in which it was to operate).

Weight loss program

Evernden turned to aircraft construction techniques to achieve the necessary weight reduction, using sheet metal gussets instead of heavy wrought iron bracketwork, and a plywood and metal sandwich construction for the vertical panels. The construction of each of the three bodies was entrusted to a different coachbuilder; 15EX went to Hooper, 16EX to Barker, and 17EX was bodied by a well-known maker of sporting bodywork, Jarvis of Wimbledon, whose distinguished clientèle included speed king Sir Malcolm Campbell and Bentley's backer Woolf Barnato.

The first of the three, 15EX, was completed early in 1928 and used for high-speed testing on the Continent, but was written off in an accident, while 16EX was completed in September of that year and shown to Edward, Prince of Wales,

when he visited Rolls-Royce the same month; "No sale was effected," lamented Evernden, but the car—with an estimated price ticket in the region of £2,850 (almost $13,000 at the then rate of exchange)—soon found an owner, a Mr. Fuller of Ealing, though he quickly sold the car, doubtless for a swift profit, to a well-known sporting motorist named Captain J. F. C. Kruse.

"RUNNING BOARDS RESEMBLED THE FLOATS OF THE VICTORIOUS SCHNEIDER TROPHY SUPERMARINE"

A more exalted destiny awaited 17EX, which was completed in the autumn of 1928 and sold for a discounted price of 42,000 rupees ($9,150) in December 1928 to the 33-year-old Maharaja Hari Singh Bahadur, ruler of the princely state of Jammu and Kashmir in India, whose family was said to own no fewer than 26 Rolls-Royce motorcars, doubtless the reason for the discounted price. The Anglophile Maharajah had served as a Page of Honor to the Viceroy of India, Lord Curzon of Kedleston, at the grand 1911 Delhi Durbar that celebrated the accession of King George V of England as Emperor of India. When his father had died in 1909, the British Raj had taken a close interest in the education of the ruler-in-waiting, who had received an upper-crust military training with the Imperial Cadet Corps at Dehra Dun and become Commander-in-Chief of the Jammu and Kashmir state forces at the age of 20.

The car, which incorporated many departures from standard, including an engine positioned 1.5 inches further forward than the normal position and a shortened steering column, had been extensively road-tested at Derby before being shipped to its new owner's mountainous domain. It had a reported 4,350 miles on the clock, half of it covered before the body was fitted, and had apparently recorded 99.5 hp on the bench with an open exhaust.

Distinct features

Among its special features were a solid cover over the rear seats to enhance the streamlining; this could be deployed to provide a cover for the legs of the occupants of the rear seats, the rear section hinging back to create their backrest. The rear seats also had their own windshield, and were included beneath the shelter of the disappearing top. The aerofoil section combined running boards and tool boxes on either side resembled the floats of the victorious Schneider Trophy Supermarine seaplanes that owed their winning performance to their specially developed Rolls-Royce "R" aero engines.

17EX marked the end of Rolls-Royce's experiments with open sports cars. There were two reasons for this; firstly, the introduction of the Phantom II in the fall of 1929, with a new chassis whose semi-elliptic rear suspension called for a chassis frame that extended to the rear spring shackles, made it difficult to build a body with a long and elegant tail like those fitted to the cantilever-sprung experimental Phantom I sports tourers. And secondly, tourer bodies were rapidly becoming unfashionable, thanks to the development of the sports saloon, whose

better aerodynamic shape enabled it to provide similar performance to the open car despite its greater frontal area. A further bonus of the closed sports body was that it was more rigid than the open tourer, which was prone to develop stress cracks around the door openings. Despite its performance, 17EX had proved a blind alley as far as the development of new models was concerned.

The Maharaja kept 17EX until 1932, when he is recorded as having sold the car to one Ram Narain of Kanpur, in the state of Uttar Pradesh. He only retained 17EX for a few months before parting with it to a prominent connoisseur of very exclusive automobiles, P. K. Mitter of Calcutta, who also owned a Duesenberg and an Isotta Fraschini. Mitter drove 17EX for some 11 years before selling it to Greta Devi of Allahabad in 1944. A West Bengal registration document dated 1956 indicates a transfer of ownership between one Sukosh Banerjee and Bimal Kanti Ghose, both of Calcutta, but the next long-term owner was the Raja Saheb of the remote princely state of Bhadri, in the north central province of Madhya Pradesh.

Some 10 years later, around 1967, news of the car's existence reached the ear of a keen collector named Pratap Roy, Maharajkumar of Santosh, who already owned a 1928 Hooper-bodied Phantom I and a Mercedes-Benz 540K. He eventually persuaded the Raja Saheb to part with 17EX, which was in poor shape "after years of being locked up in a dark garage." Part of the deal was a request for Roy to help the Raja Saheb, a keen dog lover, find a pair of corgis!

Roy restored and enjoyed 17EX, but eventually the car had to be sold to finance the purchase of a new addition to his collection, and in 1976 it was acquired by British dealer Christopher Renwick, who arranged to have the car shipped to Europe. There it was sold to two Italian collectors, Dr. Veniero Molari, a Fiat executive, and Giulio Vignale, nephew of the famous *carrozziere*.

During the 1990s, the car was entrusted to Gianni Pena, a modeler for the leading Torinese coachbuilders, for restoration, which was still ongoing when 17EX was acquired by Victor Müller, CEO of the Spyker supercar company. Since restoration was completed, the car won the Trofeo Rolls-Royce for the most elegant example of the marque at the Villa d'Este Concours in 1996, and appeared at Pebble Beach as part of the celebration of the 100th anniversary of the Rolls-Royce company in 2004.

Owned by Austrian Alexander Schaufler since 2009, 17EX looks every inch as elegant as it did almost 80 years ago when it was delivered to Maharaja Hari Singh Bahadur. Once described as resembling some extraterrestrial dragonfly, the car is a unique testament to the thrill, beauty, and brilliance of the Rolls-Royce Phantom in all of its guises.

Special thanks to Bonhams for providing text and color photography for this article

Previous pages: 17EX's features include its disappearing top and rear windshield

Opposite: The experimental model's distinctive frontal profile

ON TOP DOWN UNDER

A five-day road trip across New South Wales in Australia shows just why the Phantom II cemented Rolls-Royce's status as a world-beater

WORDS BY DAVID BERTHON

In addition to selling remarkably well in a very difficult economic climate, the Phantom II further defined Rolls-Royce as "the best car in the world" at a time when several other marques seriously challenged for this title. The model not only introduced many advances upon its launch, but also evolved over the course of its six-year production run, with no fewer than 60 major changes to its specification between 1929 and 1935.

A most imposing car

More than 8.1 m long in chassis form and weighing over 2,500 kg, the standard Phantom II is a big car by any measure, and perhaps the most imposing of all prewar Rolls-Royces. Visually, the model introduced a much lower stance compared with the Phantom I. Its traditional radiator with vertical shutters was closer to the ground and extended well below the chassis line, which meant that the car lent itself to some rather exotic coachwork.

Mechanically, the Phantom II differed from its predecessor in a number of important areas. The biggest change was to the transmission, which was now in unit with the engine and also had an enclosed flywheel and an open propeller shaft in lieu of a heavy torque tube. The torque was taken through semi-elliptic, underslung rear springs rather than cantilever-type ones. Final drive was through a fully floating rear axle with hypoid drive, which, together with the underslung springs, enabled Henry Royce to lower the overall chassis height.

The Phantom II's ignition was dual, by magneto and coil, while the six-cylinder engine retained the same bore and stroke as the Phantom I—with a capacity of 7,668 cc —but was redesigned by Royce with a cross-flow aluminum cylinder head. As before, the carburetor was his design, too, with the Company declaring: "Rolls-Royce Ltd. have at all times found it necessary to produce a carburetor of their own design in order to obtain the requisite high standard of flexibility combined with fuel economy." Despite this, the V12 engine in the Phantom III—which was introduced in 1936, three years after Royce had passed away— employed a Stromberg design.

The Phantom was continually modified. Among its many updates were thermostatic shutters added to the radiator, extra cylinder lubrication, a wider front track, improved front brakes, one-shot chassis lubrication, heavier exhaust valves, synchromesh on third and top gear, a larger 28-gallon fuel tank, stronger clutch springs, and one-inch-smaller 20-inch wheels, which were later reduced to 19 inches.

The defining version

Yet, what arguably defined the Phantom II most was the short-chassis Continental sports version introduced in 1931.

Whereas most long-chassis cars carried formal coachwork and were designed to be chauffeur-driven, the Continental was primarily for the owner-driver and generally featured

Opposite, from top: Of the six Phantom II Continentals now in Australia, this 1933 Fernandez and Darrin short-coupled saloon (106PY) carries what is surely the most exotic coachwork; the subject of David's road test, 86PY, which was ordered with three spare wheels—one on each side and one aft—perhaps in recognition of the long distances between towns in Australia

Right, from top: Sketches by Ivan Evernden, dated April 10, 1930, for the body of the first Phantom II Continental, 26EX; intended for Henry Royce's personal use, the second Phantom II Continental, 27EX, had a Park Ward body that was a carbon copy of its Barker predecessor

Opposite: Gurney Nutting made some wonderful Phantom II Continentals, including this coupe on 94MY

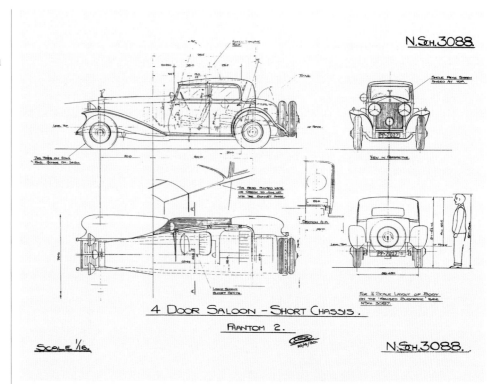

N.SCH. 3088.

4 DOOR SALOON — SHORT CHASSIS.

PHANTOM 2.

SCALE ⅟16.

N.SCH. 3088.

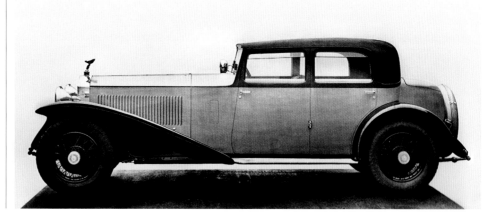

close-coupled coachwork. The radiator mounted just behind the front-axle line, with a long tapered hood leading up to a windscreen located more or less amidships, gives the car a very sporty line. The driver sits well back behind a low-raked steering column, meaning that—with the rear passengers positioned in front of the rear axle—the chassis space devoted to the compartment behind him is very short indeed. Despite this, those at the back have more than adequate legroom, helped by recessed foot wells in the floor.

The Continental is some 150 mm shorter than the standard version of the Phantom II, and its coachwork is more compact. As a result, the car is lighter, and being lower, too, due to reset springs, it cuts through the air far better than the long-wheelbase vehicles, with their taller, more expansive bodies. Admittedly, the Continental is not very space-efficient for such a large car, but the size of the rear compartment was, of course, not the main priority for the owner-driver. The overall effect is stunningly elegant, and in the early 1930s, nothing came close for fast, quiet, long-distance touring.

The test of time

A few years ago, in 2006, I was fortunate enough to be able to see for myself if the Phantom II Continental has stood the test of time. I had already driven Barrie and Margaret Gillings' impressive 1930 Hooper landaulette de ville, chassis 147GN, on a number of occasions, so when the opportunity arose to drive a rare Continental, I jumped at it.

Only 21 Phantoms II were imported into Australia in the 1930s, as the country suffered

during the Great Depression. Of those, just five were the sportier Continental type—including chassis 86PY, which I was going to drive.

The Rolls-Royce records show that the car was off test in October 1933 and fitted with an H. J. Mulliner Weymann sports saloon body. Two months later in London, it was delivered to Sir Warwick Fairfax, Managing Director of John Fairfax & Sons (now John Fairfax Holdings Ltd.), the publisher of *The Sydney Morning Herald*. He then shipped 86PY to Sydney in August 1934, where it remained with his family until purchased from his widow in 2002.

Sir Warwick sent this highly original car—one of his favored ones—to the factory in 1967 and had it totally refurbished, at a cost rumored to have equaled that of a then new Silver Shadow. On its return to Australia, he used 86PY sparingly, and the current owner again shipped it to the UK—to specialists Ristes Motor Company—for further mechanical restoration in 2002. As a result, the car is in superb overall condition and must surely rank as one of the best of the six Phantom II Continentals known to be Down Under at present.

User-friendly

My test drive was a five-day trip to Orange in New South Wales, where I was to attend the 2006 Federal Rally of the Rolls-Royce Owners' Club of Australia. The climb up over the Blue Mountains provided a chance for some good long-legged motoring on fast-moving but at times undulating roads, and on the highway out of Sydney, the added refinement of the Phantom II chassis was immediately apparent.

The half-elliptic springs gave a distinctly more "sporting" feel and certainly made for a firmer, more controlled ride with less tendency to "float" at speed than the Phantom I, with its long semi-elliptic springs and poor damping control. The handling and steering also felt noticeably more modern than in the earlier cars and far lighter at speed than I'd expected,

"THE CONTINENTAL IS VERY COMFORTABLE INDEED, WITH SUFFICIENT MODERN FEATURES TO MAKE IT VERY USABLE IN TODAY'S TRAFFIC"

particularly in comparison with the early long-wheelbase Phantom II, which can be a bit of a handful.

The Continental's smooth steering was down to a special rig Royce had developed to "run in" steering boxes. However, relatively high-geared, it is susceptible to "tram line." My test car also proved sensitive to changes in road camber, which are very much part of our country roads. In fairness, though, this condition was exacerbated by a new set of Dunlop tires with sharp edges.

According to *The Motor* magazine, the Phantom II's worm-and-nut steering was "the lightest [they] had come across in any type of car." Without a doubt, it is far more manageable at low speeds than a Duesenberg, Hispano-Suiza, or Isotta Fraschini of the period, and perhaps it is this feature alone that makes the Phantom II user-friendlier as a collector car.

Near perfection
By the time 86PY had been built, Continentals had gained some new performance features, including a semi-expanding carburetor, a high-lift camshaft, and a higher compression ratio of 5.25 to 1. However, the high-lift camshaft proved a disappointment, as the cam profile led to excessive wear and noise, eventually causing the tappets to break up. Unsurprisingly, in 1935, the lower-profile camshaft was reinstated and retrofitted to the earlier high-lift engines.

Other updates included on 86PY were a silent second gear, a heavier Nitralloy crankshaft, cast-iron brake drums, ride control via Hartford friction shock absorbers, and optional Andre Telecontrol hydraulic shock dampers. This last addition must have been a sensation in 1933, for on rough surfaces they are most effective at keeping the unsprung weight of two rather heavy axles planted firmly on the road. They automatically adjust the damping action to suit road speed, but you can choose your own setting with the central lever located on the steering hub.

That same year, Royce's servo-assisted brakes were also near perfection—powerful, with good progressive pedal pressure, and free of squealing, which is very much a characteristic of late four-wheel-brake Silver Ghosts and Phantoms I. Two years later, in 1935, Rolls-Royce added synchromesh to second gear, a large choke carburetor, and flexible engine mountings. While the syncro would certainly have made the car easier to drive, especially in fast-moving traffic, the flexibility in third gear is such that second is rarely needed. On the whole, the right-hand gearshift is easy to use, as it is more defined without the clumsy notched gate of the earlier cars and much lighter in operation.

Hitting top speed
Whereas the Phantom I starts to run out of steam at around 70 mph, its successor is

Above: One of the most handsome of all the Continentals was 43GX, coachbuilt in 1930 by the Belgian firm Van den Plas for Baron Jean Empain of Belgium

Opposite: 86PY—in excellent condition to this day

able to power on to nearly 80 mph, helped by improved breathing from the cross-flow head that lifts maximum revs by around 250 to 3,000. According to *The Autocar*, the Continental's higher final-drive ratio of 3.41 to 1 gave it a top-speed potential of around 92 mph, with maximum speeds in the intermediate gears of 70, 45, and 25 mph.

Although I found it hard to match that result without the benefit of the exhaust cutout on *The Autocar*'s test car, I did manage 85 mph on a long, flat straight. Yet to me it was the

Continental's uncanny ability to come down from this speed and idle along in top gear with no fuss at just 5 mph that was most impressive. I always think it is a tribute to Royce's design ingenuity that his cars display such superb flexibility in top gear.

It is also very easy to make this model flow on the open road, while being able to run up to 70 mph in third gear makes it ideal for cruising. As a touring car, the Continental is very comfortable indeed, with enough of a vintage feel to give it real character, but also

a sufficient number of modern features to make it very usable in today's traffic.

86PY had been superbly prepared for my long weekend sojourn. It benefits from the larger 28-gallon fuel tank that Sir Warwick had fitted for his extensive interstate trips. Yet despite its weight, I still managed around 13.5 mpg over 560 miles, with some fairly hard hill climbing along the way. This just goes to show that, even today, the Phantom II Continental stands out as one of the truly great cars of its era, worthy of having carried on the title of "the best car in the world."

CONTINENTAL IN AMERICA

Arguably the most desirable of all Rolls-Royce models, the
Phantom II Continental was initially ignored in North America,
but went on to win over many collectors

WORDS BY ANDRÉ BLAIZE

If you think the Phantom II Continental is the Holy Grail of Rolls-Royce cars, you are probably not too far off the truth. However, this has not always been the case, and there was a time not too long ago when this extraordinary model could have been snapped up for a relatively modest amount of money.

Greater prestige

When the Phantom II replaced the New Phantom in 1929, it was a real improvement in terms of performance, comfort, and prestige. So, it is no surprise that more than 120 of the 1,767 Phantoms II produced were sold to North America, even though the Great Depression —which ultimately led to the closure of the Rolls-Royce plant at Springfield, Massachusetts in 1931—did not encourage the incurring of that sort of expense.

These sales figures prove that Americans were still eager to buy the marque. The Phantom II's left-hand-drive chassis series AJS and AMS were particularly popular, but if you wanted a very exclusive car with a sportier appearance, a short-wheelbase Continental—launched in 1931—was the one to have.

Fewer than 300 of all Phantoms II built were ordered as Continentals. However, given that North America has always been a prime market for Rolls-Royce, it is still hard to believe that just a single Phantom II Continental was delivered to the USA—and even that was two years after the model had been launched!

A short-lived adventure

That car was chassis 186MY, a right-hand-drive model bought by Captain John Wanamaker of New York City and Philadelphia, Pennsylvania. Born in Paris on August 1, 1890, he was a film producer who'd previously owned Silver Ghost 7YG—which carried a cabriolet body by Hooper—before switching to New Phantom 82NC, also a cabriolet but bodied by Barker. He took delivery of his Continental 186MY in September 1933 but passed away the following year in New York City at the age of 44.

Consequently, the car's US adventure was short-lived and it found its way back to the UK, where Conservative Party politician Sir Terence James O'Connor bought it. 186MY didn't cross the Atlantic again until 1959. This time, the car remained there for half a century until an RREC member gave it a new home in Switzerland in the late 2000s.

Belated popularity

Long after that pioneering Phantom II Continental had left the New World, at least 163 used ones were sold to America—nearly 60 percent of the total built. Many of these sales were completed between the 1960s and the 1980s. There were several reasons for this trend.

For one, nobody in the UK wanted to buy a vehicle that was in less than average condition, while on the other hand, the global energy crisis of the 1970s wasn't kind to cars that got hardly more than eight miles to the gallon. Some English owners also did not realize their Continentals were rare and were too anxious to get rid of them if the price seemed decent, rather than spending loads of money on the restoration of gas guzzlers.

Prices were therefore extremely low, and since the collecting craze had just started in America, European marques crossed the Atlantic by the dozen. A few American collectors had their Continentals restored, while others simply stored them as retirement projects. If an engine needed a new head or block, or if the wood frame had to be replaced, cars were often put aside for decades. Some have only recently come out of their involuntary retirement, and quite a few are being repatriated to the UK, where, however belatedly, they have become the darlings of discerning collectors with a comfortable bank account.

Previous pages: (Left-hand page from top) 1933 Barker drophead sedanca coupe 186MY, which was entered in the prestigious Villa d'Este Concours at Lake Como, Italy by its Swiss owner in 2011; this photograph was taken in the late 1980s, when 186MY was residing in Washington State; (right-hand page) the same car when owned by R. H. Zinn in 1959/60, during its second stint on American soil

Right, from top: 208AMS, Park Ward saloon; 209AMS, a Hooper saloon with division

Opposite: 119RY, a Park Ward standard saloon, in London

THE LEFT-HAND-DRIVE MODELS

Initially, the left-hand-drive Phantoms II were destined for the American market, as denoted by the prefix A that was added to the series JS and MS. (In the same manner, the US-made Silver Ghosts and New Phantoms had carried the prefix S for Springfield.) Among the left-hand-drive Phantom II Continentals are:

- 286AJS, which was ordered by His Excellency Harry Wessel, a Danish minister and ambassador to Chile. He only used the car outside the UK, which made a left-hand-drive chassis more appropriate. Like so many other Continentals, 286AJS spent some 20 years in the USA. It then returned to Denmark in 1994, when it was acquired by Jørgen Strøyer Hansen, the famous car collector and museum owner. He also owns Continentals 8JS and 16MY.

- 207AMS, which was delivered to Baron Böcklin von Böcklinsau of Zurich, Switzerland in May 1932.

The chassis was originally fitted with a bespoke Barker saloon, but in 1934, for unknown reasons, coachbuilder Vanvooren of Courbevoie, France put a saloon with division on it. The car still survives in the USA, where it is being restored.

- 208AMS, which, although ordered by Albert Y. Gowen of Boston, Massachusetts, bore a UK registration and was delivered to Holland for his use on the Continent. It was soon sold to a British captain; however, there is no need to feel bad for Gowen—he also owned 92PY (see American Customers Abroad on following page). 208AMS went to the USA c. 1964, only to return to the Old World in 2007.

- 209AMS, which was bought new by the Marqués de Melín of Spain. In 1939, it passed to José Falcó y Álvarez de Toledo, 16th Conde de Elda, who was part of the same family. It seems that the car did not survive the Second World War because it has not been seen or heard of since 1945.

AMERICAN CUSTOMERS ABROAD

Several American millionaires who had interests in Europe bought Phantom II Continentals but never shipped them to the USA:

• 24MS was ordered by George A. Schenley of Pittsburgh, Pennsylvania and Isle of Purbeck, Dorset, UK. The chassis cards read "car for use in the UK, but mainly on Continent for fast touring." It remained in the UK until at least 1996, when it was sold by dealer Terry Cohn. Its current whereabouts are unknown.

• 92PY belonged to the same Albert Gowen who purchased 208AMS. His firm, Alpha Cement Ltd., had offices in Cleveland Square, London, so he kept 92PY there. It was strictly for use in the UK, while the Holland-based left-hand Continental 208AMS was his preferred mode of transport for excursions on the Continent. In 2012, BMW Group Classic acquired 92PY for its Rolls-Royce collection after the death of the car's previous owner, Sir James A. Cayzer.

• Corlette Glorney of New York ordered 94PY, but he only used it "in the UK, mainly for touring." The guarantee was issued on March 24, 1934, and it changed hands in February 1938. After the Second World War, the car went to South Africa, where it remained for some time with a famous car collector. It is not known when the Windovers saloon coachwork gave way to a breakdown-truck body, but that's how 94PY was found abandoned in California. It is now waiting for a new body by Australian master coachbuilder Roger Fry. Photos of the new body in the making indicate that it will be a replica of the coveted Owen drophead sedanca coupe—a specialty of Fry's.

• John B. Snow bought 119RY and had it delivered to his London address in Maida Vale. It was registered AYO869, and when he traded it for a new Phantom III (3AZ152) in 1937, it was sold to Alfred Chester-Beatty of Ashford, Kent.

A book by the writer, titled Rolls-Royce: The Phantom II Continental and published by Dalton Watson Fine Books, is due for release in June 2015

FIT FOR A PRINCESS

Like all Phantoms IV, the car commissioned for Princess Margaret is a grand affair with a tale to tell—one that spans from Clarence House, via Pennsylvania, to Liechtenstein

WORDS BY JOHN LEWIS

Imagine you're a princess. You're at the center of your own little social circle—the Margaret set—holding court at countless parties and balls around London. With dazzling blue eyes and a 24-inch waist, you're regarded as one of Europe's most beautiful royals.

Then in 1952, aged 22, your dad dies, and your sister becomes queen. It's a bit of a shock to the system. To cheer you up, your big sister decides to buy you a car. Not just any car, but one of the rarest, grandest, heaviest, and most expensive cars that have ever been built.

A unique Rolls-Royce

"It is a driver's dream," says Dr. Norbert Seeger, the Liechtenstein-based collector who has owned Princess Margaret's old Phantom IV, chassis 4BP7, for the past seven years. "It is an extremely heavy car, weighing more than 3.3 tons, so you have to take care at speeds when cornering. But it has superb roadholding, the controls are magnificent, and it fulfills every aspect of what you would expect of a Phantom IV."

For Dr. Seeger, who owns 27 exquisite Rolls-Royce and Bentley models dating back over a century, this Phantom IV represents the jewel in his collection. "The collection began in the early 1990s when I received a Silver Cloud III as a result of a defaulted mandate," he says. "By 2005, the question arose—in which direction do I go with this collection? I decided to try to get the complete Phantom set. Of course, the bottleneck for such a goal is the Phantom IV."

The Phantom IV is, of course, the most exclusive model of Rolls-Royce ever produced. Only 18 were ever made, all for royalty and state leaders, and they very rarely come on the market.

"We did a lot of relation management around the world—in Switzerland, in England, in America—over the years," he says, "and one day we came across 4BP7 and had the chance to buy it. Phantoms IV are difficult to buy and expensive to maintain, and they are always sought after by collectors. If one comes on the market, in whatever condition, it is snapped up very quickly. According to a prestigious automobile valuer in London, you would expect to pay around £900,000, or $1.4 million, for one. A Phantom IV that belonged to the royal family is even rarer."

The marque of royalty

It would appear that the Phantom IV, more than any other model, cemented the royal family's link with Rolls-Royce. Initially, it was Daimler that was awarded the Royal Warrant in 1902 and retained that role for more than half a century, despite the fact that members of the royal household had privately purchased 21 Rolls-Royce vehicles before the Second World War. But, by the time of Queen Elizabeth's succession in 1952, the royals had shifted preference, and Rolls-Royce supplanted Daimler's Royal Warrant in 1955.

In 1948, before his wife had become queen, Prince Philip, The Duke of Edinburgh, test-drove an experimental Mark V Bentley with a straight-eight engine. In November of that year,

Opposite: Princess Margaret's Phantom IV takes to the road in Liechtenstein

Philip and Elizabeth placed a private order for a Rolls-Royce limousine with similar characteristics.

The first Phantom IV, chassis 4AF2, was delivered to the coachbuilders H. J. Mulliner in July 1949 and was eventually presented to Philip and Elizabeth a year later. It certainly shared many characteristics with the Mark V Bentley. Like the Bentley, it had been hand-built at Clan Foundry, Rolls-Royce's wartime factory in Belper, Derbyshire, and shared the same straight-eight engine—powerful but able to travel long distances at a low speed, as was customary for ceremonial cars. It became the official state car when Elizabeth became queen in 1952, and is still used for state occasions—the same car transported Charles and Camilla from Clarence House to Westminster Abbey for the wedding of Kate and William in 2011.

That initial Phantom IV, codenamed "Nabha" by Rolls-Royce workers, remained a one-off for several months. Indeed, the second Phantom IV—chassis 4AF4, coachbuilt by Park Ward in October 1950—was more of a utility vehicle with a truck-like body, and was dismantled in 1963. But the subsequent models established the Phantom IV as the most exclusive Rolls-Royce ever made.

Of the 17 extant Phantoms IV, five went to the British royal family, three went to Spanish dictator General Franco, three to the Emir of Kuwait, two to the Shah of Iran, two to the Iraqi royal family, and one each to Prince Talal of Saudi Arabia and the Ishmaili Shi'ite leader Aga Khan III.

By the time Margaret's Phantom IV was commissioned by the princess's secretary —in the autumn of 1953—production had shifted from Derbyshire to Crewe in Cheshire. The resultant car, 4BP7, was given the code-name of "The Baron Montaigne." It was the largest private vehicle then being built in Britain. The princess made specifications to the coachbuilders H. J. Mulliner on January 4, 1954, and the car was delivered on July 16 to Clarence House, where Princess Margaret lived with the Queen Mother.

"THESE CARS WERE NORMALLY DRIVEN BY A CHAUFFEUR, BUT THE PRINCESS WANTED TO DRIVE IT HERSELF"

A very special spec

Margaret's car differed a little from her sister's. For starters, it had a higher and more elongated fender line, and had a different statuette above the radiator grille—an alternative to the Spirit of Ecstasy. The Queen's car had two interchangeable statuettes, both designed by the British artist (and friend of the royal family) Edward Seago: when driving in England it displayed a mascot of Saint George slaying a dragon; in Scotland, it was exchanged for a lion rampant. Princess Margaret's 4BP7 also had an original Seago design, but hers was an elegant model of a rearing Pegasus.

The driver's compartment is unusually well appointed. "When we got the car we wondered why the front section was so luxurious," says Dr. Seeger. "Why are the front seats fitted in wool, not leather? These cars were normally all driven by the chauffeur, but Princess Margaret wanted to drive it herself. As a result, because it was set up for the princess, it is extremely easy to drive."

The steering wheel is daintier than usual, the steering position one inch shorter than standard, and the column rake was set as high as possible. The driver's seat has also been fitted with a small winch that allows it to be raised a few inches. According to the modifications specified by the princess's secretary, Mulliner raised the driving seat cushion and backrest and, in case they were needed, the firm provided detachable extensions to fit the brake and accelerator pedals. It also, unusually, had an automatic gearbox, a rarity for Rolls-Royce cars of its vintage.

To guarantee smooth running, Rolls-Royce used 10 nuts on the wheel discs for 4BP7, instead of the usual five, as was customary in the Silver Wraith. Furthermore, 24 holes around the hub assisted the balance. The wheel discs have five rubber cams near to the bead of the rim in order to prevent shaking noise. These measures led to an unparalleled smoothness.

"There are many anecdotes and stories that surround the vehicle," says Dr. Seeger. "When I received it, the lamp covers were removed and disclosed a second bunch of keys. It is well known that the chauffeur of the car was meticulous with regard to every aspect of the vehicle, including the keys. The spare set of keys may have been put there as a security measure in case the first set of keys were misplaced." Rumor has it, however, that the princess had the keys put there so that she could sneak out and drive the car herself without having to inform the chauffeur.

A symphony of walnut

The rear of the car is particularly luxurious, its upholstery covered with doe-brown West of England wool. At night, the interior ceiling can be tastefully illuminated by means of indirect lighting. Moveable reading lamps are mounted on the sides, should they be required. A sliding roof, controlled by the press of a button, can be moved to the required position directly above the rear seat. The floor is covered with a fluffy wool fleece and is fitted with a Persian carpet.

An electrically operated blind, mounted on the rear window, will protect the passenger, if necessary, from prying eyes. Additional blinds can be drawn out of the side panels—the operating knobs discreetly built into the right armrest.

The main passenger seat in the rear can be raised or lowered a few inches with a small winder, and the car is fitted with two face-forward occasional seats. In between them is a cabinet housing a loudspeaker grille and a heater outlet. Below that was a lidded storage compartment with a mirror set into the center armrest, although this was later removed to allow the extra passengers to move around without hitting their legs against the lower part of the cabinet. Above the cabinet is a pair of cigarette lighters, with a clock built into the division rail.

Princess Margaret famously enjoyed a tipple, and the division panel of 4BP7 features an elegant drinks cabinet, handmade in cross-banded walnut veneer. Princess Margaret would often entertain friends in her car. Her friend Jennifer Bevan recalls going on long chauffeur-driven journeys where Margaret and friends would belt out "Baby, It's Cold Outside," "C'est Si Bon," "Bewitched," "Autumn Leaves," "La Vie En Rose," and numerous showtunes. "She'd sit there in her gleaming Rolls-Royce, singing wonderfully," recounts Bevan. "I could never keep in tune."

Life after Margaret

Princess Margaret sold 4BP7 in 1967, and the blue police lamp and royal coat of arms on the Phantom IV's roof were removed and put on her Long Wheelbase Silver Shadow. The royal registration plate—PM 6450—was changed to 302 HYP and it was sold through

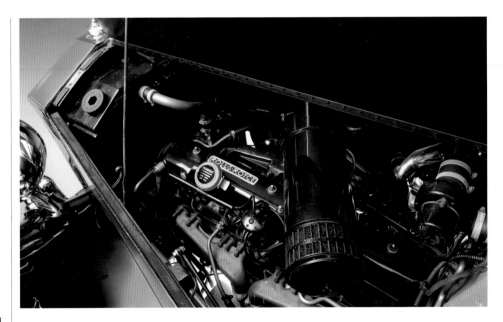

Previous pages: 4BP7, with reinstated number plate

Opposite: Edward Seago's rearing Pegasus statuette

Above: The car's powerful yet elegant straight-eight engine

"THE TRUNK WAS CHOCK-A-BLOCK WITH RADIO EQUIPMENT FOR AN EARLY CARPHONE—SOMETHING YOU ONLY EVER SEE WITH ROYAL VEHICLES"

Car Mart Dealership in Park Lane. It came to the attention of one Alfred William David Adams—better known as A. W. D. Adams and nicknamed Ben—who ran a successful transport, garage, and rental company in New Malden, Surrey, around nine miles south-west of London.

"My father had a growing collection of Rolls-Royce cars," says Graham Adams, son of A. W. D. Adams, "and our local dealership in Weybridge rang him up to tell him that they had a very unusual Rolls-Royce for sale, but they weren't able to tell us who the previous owner was. It was all a little cloak and dagger. We were quite impressed by its royal connections, but more impressed by what an extraordinary and impressive vehicle it was."

The car—which had only 27,000 miles on the clock when it was purchased in 1967—remained with the Adams family for more than three decades. "It wasn't used very often," says Graham. "We'd occasionally use it to pick up prestigious clients from Heathrow Airport, or to attend special events in London. Sometimes we'd lend it to clients or business partners we trusted, for their daughter's wedding or something."

One of the clients who occasionally borrowed 4BP7 was a firm called Farmcroft in New Malden, who would use it for films and TV shows. As a result, it appears, briefly, in a chase sequence in episode 13 of the TV series *Man In A Suitcase*, broadcast in 1968. It also appears in the 1969 James Bond film *On Her Majesty's Secret Service*, parked outside the house of M, played by Bernard Lee.

But, generally, the car was displayed in the New Malden showroom of Adams & Adams transport firm. "That was until we ran out of showroom space," says Graham, "and moved it into a heated warehouse. By this time the West of England cloth was looking a little shabby. One of our tenants was unable to pay rent, but he was an expert upholsterer—we got him to reupholster the car in lieu of rent! But that was the only work we did to it—we overhauled the engine before selling it, but never touched the paintwork."

A change of owner

By the turn of the century, A. W. D. Adams had died and the family was looking to sell its

Below: 4BP7's slender steering wheel enabled the princess to easily handle the 3.3-ton vehicle

Opposite: The car's walnut veneer division panel and well-appointed drinks cabinet

Phantom IV. "To be honest, we didn't really drive it that much," says Graham. "It was light on the steering and was nicely balanced, but it was a beast of a car to drive around town. And you did feel a bit like a chauffeur driving it."

He approached the Rolls-Royce and Bentley specialists P&A Wood to sell the car. "It didn't need much work," says Paul Wood, one of the twins who runs the dealership in Great Dunmow, Essex. "It needed a touch of paintwork, and I remember working on the corrosion around the rear wheel spats. But it was in very good condition. I've worked on a couple of other Phantoms IV: King Hussein of Jordan's one, coachbuilt by Hooper, had to be restored from the chassis up—it was one of the best restorations we've ever done. And the Aga Khan's one is currently being completely rebuilt in America. But Princess Margaret's car was in very good condition indeed."

One extraordinary feature of the car, says Paul, was the radio equipment that enabled the princess to operate an early car phone. "The trunk was chock-a-block with radio equipment for an early carphone," he says. "There was a massive receiver, valves, amplifiers, all sorts—something you only ever see with royal vehicles."

The US connection

Adams bought the car in 1967 for around £3,250—that's around £52,000, or $80,000, in today's money, allowing for inflation. He sold it through P&A Wood in 2003 for an impressive £136,000. It was bought by American collector Bob Shaffner in Pennsylvania, who had made his fortune selling aerospace parts and already

owned another Phantom IV, 4BP3, the former Prince Regent of Iraq's car. He would acquire yet another, the incomparable Aga Khan car 4AF20—making him the only person other than General Franco to have ever owned three Phantoms IV at the same time. In 2004—the Company's centenary year—Bob was invited to present Princess Margaret's car at the Pebble Beach concours where it shared the green with its former stablemate 4BP3, which he had sold on by then.

That was up until 2008, when 4BP7 was bought from The Real Car Company in North Wales by Dr. Seeger. "When I purchased the car, I was able, with special permission, to re-register the original number plate PM 6450," he says.

"The car is registered and driven regularly, as all my cars are, in order to prevent standing damage," he adds. "I try to move the prewar cars at least twice a year and the postwar cars at least every two months."

At the time of writing, the car has 64,162 miles on the clock. "It drives perfectly," says Dr. Seeger. "We use it a lot for picnics: from time to time we invite a small group of people and use three or four cars and go out locally into the countryside. It's impressive to drive the cars and especially the Phantom IV, people are always stunned to see it. When sitting in the rear and being chauffeur-driven, it inspires a feeling of majesty—as it should do."

So, would Dr. Seeger ever consider selling it on? "That," he says, quite firmly, "is totally out of the question."

Special thanks to Dr. Norbert Seeger and the Seeger Collection (www.seeger.li) for providing photography

Opposite, from top: The Phantom IV's luxurious passenger compartment, with controls for radios, lights, windows, heating, ventilation, sliding roof, and blinds; 4BP7 in all of its regal splendor

BENTLEY'S LE MANS LEGACY

The North American driver John Duff placed Bentley firmly on the racing grid at the inaugural 24 Hours of Le Mans—establishing a sporting reputation that lives on to this day

WORDS BY GRAEME COCKS

When racing driver John Duff approached Bentley's first sales manager, A. F. C. Hillstead, in 1923 with the idea of a quick sojourn to France to contest a new race he'd heard about, W. O. Bentley was famously reluctant to support his entry. Although he never questioned Duff's resolve as a driver, he thought him somewhat "pushy" and wrote in his autobiography that "Duff was a very persuasive man who was used to getting his own way." Eventually, he got it here, too.

Foreign adventures

W. O. had a long racing history of his own that extended back to before the First World War, but his cars had only taken part in competitions in the British Isles since 1921, when the first customer car had been delivered in September and limited production had been underway.

The following year, a Bentley team consisting of driver W. Douglas Hawkes and two "mechanicians" (as they were called by the American press) had crossed the Atlantic to Indianapolis for the 500-mile race in late May, where Hawkes had qualified at 81.9 mph to start in 19th position before advancing to a disappointing 13th place at race end. In retrospect, it was probably a good result, but W. O. admitted later that it had been a costly exercise that hadn't yielded the rewards he'd wanted. He said his car had just not been fast enough for Indy, and Bentley Motors had always been strapped for cash. So it was not surprising that he was less than enthusiastic about Duff's proposal for another foreign adventure, this time at Le Mans in France.

His factory cars had not yet ventured to the Continent to compete. They had raced at Brooklands and at various hill climbs in the British Isles, and enjoyed favorable reviews. The greatest performance to date had been at the International Tourist Trophy Race, the TT, on the Isle of Man in June 1922, where Bentley had won the team prize in appalling, wet conditions. The publicity had been valuable, and the "Race on Sunday, sell on Monday" principle was by now well established.

Duff may have cited this principle to press his case regarding Le Mans. Plus, on September 27, 1922, a few months after the TT result, he had delivered the fledgling Bentley company a great deal of prestige by securing the European Double Twelve-Hour Record of 2,082 miles in 24 hours at Brooklands with his personal car, chassis 141.

Although people often assume he was British, Duff was, in fact, Canadian—born in China to Canadian parents and then raised and educated in Canada. Nevertheless, he'd enlisted in the British Army and settled in England after the war, becoming a car dealer in London. During this period, he'd developed a love for motorsport that married happily with his dealership for Bentley cars.

A race against time

The concept of a race over 24 hours was not new. Even though today Le Mans is acclaimed

Previous pages: Chassis 141 takes to the grid at the start of the 1923 Le Mans

Above: S. F. Edge puts the Napier through its paces for the 1907 24-hour record

Opposite: Bentley's famous entrant before the inaugural endurance race

as the first 24-hour race for sports cars, automobilists had been racing against the clock—and each other—over the course of an entire day since 1905. That year, Charles G. Wridgway drove a 24 hp Peerless on New York's Brighton Beach track with the aim of covering 1,000 miles in 24 hours. He only managed 923 miles but kept driving and passed the 1,000-mile mark in 25 hours and 50 minutes. A short time later at the Empire City Race Track in New York, Guy Vaughan set a 24-hour record of 1,015 miles in a 40 hp Decauville.

It wasn't until July 1907 that a 24-hour record was set in Europe. Selwyn Francis Edge, the effervescent Australian-born marketer of Napier cars, claimed it at the newly opened Brooklands track near London. At the time, he was quoted as saying: "What I want to prove is that an ordinary touring motorcar, in its present state of perfection, can run for 24 consecutive hours at 60 miles an hour without the driver having anything to do but guide it. The experiment will show that the modern motorcar is the fastest thing that has ever moved on Earth."

He even exceeded his target of driving a mile a minute for 24 hours (1,440 miles in total) by recording 1,581 miles in a day, at an average speed of almost 66 mph.

The first Le Mans

However, all of these accomplishments were endurance records rather than races. The first 24-hour race was run at Columbus, Ohio in July 1905 in front of a crowd of 15,000 spectators. Four cars contested the event, and a Pope-Toledo driven by Charles and George Soules won

it, covering 828.5 miles. At St. Paul, Minnesota in June 1907, Rafaelo Mongini managed over 200 miles more in a 24-hour race at the Hamlin track, claiming a world record by driving 1,037 miles.

These races and others like them attracted enormous crowds. At Brighton Beach track in September 1908, 20,000 people witnessed Ralph Mulford beating 10 other cars and increasing the distance mark to 1,107 miles in 24 hours in a six-cylinder 50 hp Lozier.

"DESPITE THE FRUSTRATION OF POOR BRAKING, THE BENTLEY SET THE INAUGURAL LAP RECORD"

The concept of a 24-hour race to promote the attributes of ordinary touring cars was revived by the Automobile Club de l'Ouest at Le Mans, France in 1923, and the event has survived to the present day. The circuit hosted many other races prior to 1923, including Jimmy Murphy's famous Duesenberg victory in 1921, when the American entered the 15th French Grand Prix and won the 322-mile, four-hour race at 78.1 mph.

John Duff and his racing partner, British driver Frank Clement, should have noted that Murphy had used hydraulic four-wheel drum brakes. The Le Mans track was extremely

rough, and pictures of the time show that it was strewn with quite large stones, so four-wheel brakes would have been a great advantage when coming up to the corners. When Clement prepared Duff's 141, all Bentleys had only two-wheel brakes on the rear, a fundamental disadvantage for the Bentley boys as their rivals were equipped with brakes on each wheel. Those used by Spanish carmaker Hispano-Suiza—the first company to offer four-wheel brakes operated by a single foot pedal in 1919—were even power-assisted.

No lucky brake

The Le Mans race turned out to be a great adventure. Two 3L French Chenard-Walcker cars came home in first and second position, the leading car covering 1,372 miles at an average speed of 57.1 mph. However, Duff and Clement were frustrated by harder-braking cars ahead, and late-braking cars behind. Also, they weren't prepared for the local conditions and lost too much time to win when they holed their fuel tank.

Despite the frustration of poor braking, the Bentley set the inaugural lap record of 67 mph. The performances at Le Mans in 1923 make an interesting comparison to S. F. Edge's 24-hour speed average on a banked track of 65.9 mph back in 1907. How cars had improved when a touring car could now drive around a rough road track at a similar speed as one of the fastest racers of 16 years before!

Remarkably, when Duff and Clement returned to Le Mans a year later—this time

"THANKS IN GREAT PART TO DUFF AND CLEMENT'S PIONEERING WORK WITH 141, BENTLEY BECAME FIRMLY ESTABLISHED AS A SPORTING CAR"

with the total commitment of W. O. Bentley—and won the race, they did it at an average speed of 53.8 mph, covering 82 miles less over the 24 hours than the winning Chenard-Walcker of the year before. Without having to repair a fuel tank that was holed—no doubt by a rock thrown up from the deteriorating track—they covered 92 miles more than in 1923.

A new passion

Chassis 141 was the beginning of the Bentley passion for Le Mans, and through that first race W. O. began to understand what was required to win the soon-to-be greatest motorcar endurance race in the world. Although the lack of four-wheel brakes was the critical limiting factor in the performance in 1923, other factors were at play. The Chenard-Walcker team led the race, and while the Bentley was never far behind, it was obvious that stock touring cars needed strengthening to survive the rigors of a 24-hour race.

The following year, they returned with wooden slats around the fuel tank to protect it from the type of damage they had sustained in 1923. Flying rocks thrown up by other cars had also knocked out both headlight lenses, so for 1924 they fitted mesh stoneguards over the headlights. These have now become a "must-have" accessory for almost every vintage Bentley. In 1924, Duff and Clement also built a toolbox into the running board (only the drivers

were allowed to work on the cars), and they carried a spare tire during the race, too.

It is no wonder, then, that W. O. said he owed the most to John Duff. Thanks in great part to his and Clement's pioneering work with 141 in 1923 and their subsequent win in 1924, Bentley sold more than 700 cars in two years and the marque became firmly established as a sporting car.

A test of survival

However, in 1925, bad luck hit the Bentley team and they could not recreate the success of the previous year. W. O. said that "healthy modesty had given way to over-confidence," adding: "As we were to discover to our cost, there is nothing so calculated to send you off on the slippery slope of failure as cocksureness in motor racing."

Le Mans has invariably been as much a test of survival as of out-and-out speed. In fact, race times had not improved greatly by 1925, and a La Lorraine recorded a similar distance over 24 hours as the winning car in the first year of the race. Unlike Grand Prix or Indy races, mechanical sophistication has not always equated to success at the French racetrack, which is evident from the excellent performances of some of the cars that are today seen as having inferior technical specifications.

For example, a Chrysler Six was in the high placings in 1925 and showed that overhead valves and an overhead camshaft were not that much more effective in those days than

Opposite (from top): The Le Mans starting line-up in 1925; chassis 141 receives some TLC after taking an overnight battering at the 24-hour race

Opposite (from top): Current owner
Peter Briggs at the wheel of chassis 141
following its restoration; the motorcar's
sorry condition prior to its rehabilitation

a flathead motor with pressure lubrication and a degree of refinement. The car, entered by Chrysler's Paris distributor St. Didier, came sixth with 1,262 miles covered in 24 hours—only about 30 miles less than Duff and Clement's winning drive a year earlier. In 1928, the trusty flathead Chryslers also came home third and fourth behind the Bentley of Barnato and Rubin, and the Stutz of Brisson and Bloch.

A formidable presence
That year, the 4½ Litre Bentley won the day at an average speed of 69 mph. The Bentley team was formidable, and with a 50 percent increase in engine capacity compared with the Bentleys raced by Duff and Clement in 1923 and 1924, it would have taken a highly organized challenger to beat them.

The team's accumulated race experience was intimidating to other carmakers. In fact, the French auto manufacturers began withdrawing from the big-car class in 1927 —an Aries was the only 3L French car that year, and it was the same in 1928. During these years, Le Mans did not see the most famous French sporting marque in the competition —a couple of Brescia Bugattis had contested the first event, but Bugatti did not return to the 24-hour race until 1930. Similarly, sports-car manufacturers such as Delage did not enter. So, the American Stutz, with its bulky OHC motor, and four Chryslers were the only competition for the Bentleys, as the 2L and smaller-displacement cars were significantly slower than the bigger ones.

Chassis 141 has a special place in Le Mans history as the first foreign entry in the race, the inaugural lap record holder and, most importantly, the car that began the Bentley fascination with the race. It was also arguably the first Bentley "team car" at Le Mans, as W. O. Bentley supported the entry and provided Frank Clement to drive with John Duff.

Incidentally, W. Douglas Hawkes, who had piloted the first Bentley at Indy, never raced a Bentley there again, but in 1926 he returned to race Ernest Eldridge's Amilcar special with an Anzani engine, retiring early with a seized camshaft. John Duff was at the same race, driving a Miller called the Elcar Special to ninth place. Although he'd raced mainly before the First World War, Hawkes really became known in the 1920s through fine drives at Brooklands and elsewhere in Europe, often for Bentley. He set and broke several speed records. Upon moving to France he ran a workshop at Montlhéry for years until financial problems led to its closure in 1936. He also ran a small engineering company in the UK where, upon his own retirement from racing, he prepared racing cars. One of his main drivers was top female driver Gwenda Stewart, whom he later married.

As for John Duff, he was inducted into the Canadian Motorsport Hall of Fame in 2006—a suitable accolade for the man who drove Bentley into the Le Mans history books. *The author, Graeme Cocks, is an Australian motor journalist and was the CEO of Perth's now-defunct Fremantle Motor Museum, which was set up by Peter Briggs, the current owner of chassis 141*

SIXTY YEARS OF STYLE

In 1955, Rolls-Royce launched two groundbreaking new models—the Silver Cloud and the S series—that would go on to become design classics

WORDS BY DAVIDE BASSOLI

A short drive from London, just past Eton College and the Queen's home at Windsor Castle, the historic village of Bray in Berkshire was the setting for the launch of two of Rolls-Royce's most celebrated models on April 22, 1955: The Rolls-Royce Silver Cloud and the Bentley S series.

Up until the Second World War, the Company had never produced a complete car (i.e. chassis with coachwork). In fact, its only consistent exterior feature had been the iconic radiator grille. But the superlative lines of the Silver Cloud standard steel saloon, magisterially designed by Chief Designer John P. Blatchley, created a well-defined identity for the marque, and the model is now widely considered to represent the Rolls-Royce in its most classic form.

Cautious change

In building this car, the Company had its eye firmly set on the lucrative American market. Many of the Silver Cloud's features —such as overall proportions, dynamic road performance, and automatic transmission as standard—were designed with this target in mind. However, despite such a forward-looking approach, it was still a traditional motorcar from a mechanical point of view, with a front-mounted engine, rear-wheel drive, drum brakes, independent suspensions to the front, and semi-elliptic leaf springs to the rear.

Likewise, despite having recently started to design its own coachwork, Crewe, unlike other manufacturers, was not yet prepared to adopt monocoque technology. Instead, it kept body and chassis construction separate until this production method was more established, since the structural stresses resulting from it were not yet fully understood.

The other reason for sticking with the tried-and-tested processes was that some clients still wanted a bespoke body. Like most other luxury carmakers, Rolls-Royce and Bentley had traditionally produced chassis only and left it to the buyer to have custom or semi-custom coachwork made by their preferred coachbuilder. By the time of the Silver Cloud era, however, only five main English coachbuilders survived —Park Ward, H. J. Mulliner, Hooper, James

Opposite: The Silver Cloud standard saloon in an early picture from 1955. The Bentley S series was fundamentally the same car but with a differently shaped radiator grille and its own badging

Below: A Bentley S1 Continental "sports saloon" by H. J. Mulliner, more commonly known as a "fastback"

Young, and Freestone & Webb. Their approach had also changed since the Second World War, as they now rarely proposed one-off designs. Instead, they focused on small runs of only a few dozen bodies and offered customers the opportunity to choose from a wide range of colors and to modify certain details according to personal taste or to fit particular equipment.

"THE COMPANY HAD ITS EYE FIRMLY SET ON THE LUCRATIVE AMERICAN MARKET"

The chassis that Rolls-Royce delivered to coachbuilders were equipped with bumpers, scuttle, dashboard instruments, trunk platform with spare wheel, and, of course, all mechanical components. The radiator grille dimensions for bespoke cars—whether Rolls-Royce or Bentley —were identical to those of the standard steel saloons, and grilles were to be fitted vertically only, not inclined, in order to maintain the important frontal aspect that defined both marques. In addition, the coachbuilders submitted all their drawings to Crewe for approval to avoid any unseemly oddities.

A new Continental
Following the earlier success of the Bentley R Type Continental, that model's chassis was offered for the S series as of the end of 1955 and made available to coachbuilders. The R Type Continental had been conceived as a completely new car with its own body, which had been created as a result of collaboration between Ivan Evernden of Rolls-Royce's Experimental Department and coachbuilder H. J. Mulliner's Technical Director,

Left: In 1958, H. J. Mulliner proposed a drophead coupe named Adaptation, which proved very successful in the United States

Following pages: (Left-hand page) Park Ward offered this magnificent drophead coupe version for the S1 Continental chassis; (right-hand page, from top) for the long wheelbase chassis, Park Ward offered a touring limousine derived from the standard steel saloon; the Silver Cloud II standard steel saloon was outwardly identical to the first series, but under the hood it had the new V8 engine

At the beginning, three different two-door body styles were offered: the H. J. Mulliner saloon, and the Park Ward saloon and drophead. In its official documentation, H. J. Mulliner referred to its coachwork as "sports saloon," but since it really was an evolution of the R Type Continental body style, it is commonly known as the "fastback."

The most important development with regard to the Continental chassis was H. J. Mulliner's introduction of a four-door body style in 1957. This new design was officially known by the charming name Flying Spur, derived from the Scottish coat of arms of the firm's Managing Director, Harry T. Johnstone. Initially, those in charge at Rolls-Royce were reluctant to agree to this body style because the S Type Continental chassis had been intended for two-door sports saloons and dropheads only. But Johnstone used his influence to persuade them otherwise because he was convinced of the coachwork's potential for opening a new niche in the market: the family car as fast transport.

When he showed the superb design to the Rolls-Royce Board of Directors, they agreed and let him proceed. Throughout its eight years of production, the Flying Spur proved him right, becoming the most successful coachbuilt model on the Silver Cloud and S Type chassis.

Model modifications

Meanwhile, the beautiful drophead coupe with a fully coachbuilt light-alloy body that H. J. Mulliner was already producing for the Silver

Stanley Watts. The S Type Continental, on the other hand, was offered as a standard chassis only.

Compared with the standard model, the new Continental had higher rear-axle and engine-compression ratios and a reduced frontal area as the radiator grille was 1.5 inches lower and the steering column more inclined. This allowed for lower and more aerodynamic bodies, which enabled these cars to reach the considerable (at least for the time) maximum speed of 120 mph.

Cloud I and S1 chassis had become ever more expensive to build over the years. In 1958, the coachbuilder therefore decided to reduce the costs of construction and tooling by using the main structure and body-pressing machine of the Crewe standard steel four-door saloon to produce a two-door model with a convertible top.

After putting some pressure on Crewe, H. J. Mulliner was able to obtain a standard body shell, unpainted, which they cut up— literally with a hacksaw—before carrying out the necessary modifications. Having to cut off the roof meant reinforcing the body at the scuttle and affixing it solidly to the chassis instead of using flexible mounts as before. The beauty of its shape and the competitive price made the drophead coupe (called Adaptation at H. J. Mulliner) one of the bestselling coachbuilt models on the Silver Cloud and S Type chassis, and its production continued until 1963.

To capitalize on the success of the standard steel saloon, Rolls-Royce introduced a long wheelbase (lwb) version of the Silver Cloud and S Type in 1957, to be offered alongside the Silver Wraith. The latter was most often a large car, frequently with limousine coachwork and intended to be chauffeur-driven. The Silver Cloud lwb, on the other hand, was conceived primarily for the owner-driver. That's how it was described in a factory brochure, which, however, also conceded that the lwb "is often used as a business car, driven by the firm's chauffeur."

Its 127-inch wheelbase—four inches longer than standard— allowed the fitting of a division between the front and rear compartments without

sacrificing any legroom at the back. The body was made by Rolls-Royce's own coachbuilder, Park Ward, which modified the standard steel bodies from Pressed Steel Co. according to the new requirements. The lwb chassis was available for coachbuilt body variants as well.

Powering into the US

In 1959, the second S series was launched at the Paris and London motor shows. Nothing had changed outwardly—the styling of the Silver Cloud II and S2 was just the same as before. The big difference was under the hood: a new V8 engine.

The main feature of this mechanical jewel was that it consisted of an aluminum block and heads—a big step forward from the old cast-iron straight-six. The new material made it lighter but also slightly noisier, necessitating the introduction of hydraulic tappets that were actuated by a single camshaft fitted in the middle of the two banks.

Rolls-Royce wasn't in the habit of disclosing power and torque figures, but contemporary road testers pegged the new V8 at about 200 hp—an increase of nearly 20 percent over the straight-six. However, it wasn't only technical reasons that had convinced the Company to build a larger engine, but commercial ones, too. Exports to the United

States were by far the most important for Crewe, and American customers had a clear preference for this number of cylinders. In fact, the V8 proved so popular in the States that most other European motorcar manufacturers with designs on that market also saw the need to build this kind of engine.

A facelift

The introduction of the V8 engine in 1959 boosted sales of Rolls-Royce and Bentley cars in every corner of the world, especially in the United States. Yet even this important mechanical change only served to stem the decline in sales

Opposite: The long wheelbase chassis was available to all independent coachbuilders. Here it is shown as an S1 Touring Limousine by James Young

Left, from top: In 1959, the S2 Continental drophead coupe by Vilhelm Koren for Park Ward introduced revolutionary styling by Rolls-Royce and Bentley standards; Koren's innovative Park Ward styling introduced on the S2 Continental chassis was also offered for the third series—here modified to work with the new twin-headlamp look

Opposite: The Silver Cloud III standard steel saloon offered in 1962 had a new frontal treatment with twin headlamps and lowered radiator grille

"THE V8 ENGINE BOOSTED SALES OF ROLLS-ROYCE AND BENTLEY CARS IN EVERY CORNER OF THE WORLD, ESPECIALLY IN THE STATES"

of this model range for two years. By then, it was only seven years old—young by Rolls-Royce standards—and having pondered the situation, the Executive Board asked the Styling Department to update the design.

Up until this point, the most important development in terms of coachwork was certainly Park Ward's drophead on the Continental chassis. Also introduced in 1959, it had been designed by the talented Vilhelm Koren, who'd joined John Blatchley's Styling Department in 1957. It had taken him only six months to come up with a plasticine quarter-scale model featuring a futuristic shape that had initially been met with a certain apprehension at Crewe. The Koren drophead coupe really was a departure from what Rolls-Royce customers had been used to, but it went on to become a great success, with 125 such bodies produced—a remarkable number.

Since the shape and proportions of the S series body had been so warmly received, the Styling Department now considered the frontal appearance of the car a promising area for introducing changes without upsetting the overall lines. Twin headlamps that were smaller than the single ones used on the two previous series therefore became the most distinctive new feature of the Silver Cloud III.

Fog lights were still fitted but no longer had a dual function as flashing indicators. Those were instead incorporated into redesigned sidelights, positioned on the front of the fenders. Cars for the home market can be recognized by the smaller bumper overriders (export models retained the larger ones), while the rear lamps now had separate orange flashing lights as introduced on the last Silver Cloud II. To complete the new appearance, the height of the radiator was reduced by about 1.5 inches, giving a sloping hood line that markedly improved forward vision.

The new twin headlamps were also used on all the coachbuilt models. However, updating the frontal aspect of Vilhelm Koren's design for the Park Ward drophead coupe proved rather complicated because its straight, modern lines did not allow a satisfying marriage with twin headlamps. The Styling Department looked to Italian cars for inspiration and positioned the lights horizontally on the front fenders. The inner headlamps were placed slightly lower than the outer ones, lending the car a somewhat peculiar, slanted frontal appearance that earned the new model the nickname Chinese Eye.

In the meantime, the big novelty at the 1963 London Motor Show was the introduction of coachbuilt bodies for the Silver Cloud III chassis, since they had previously been reserved for the Continental chassis only. The radiator grille with its Greek-temple shape elegantly matched the sporty lines produced by the coachbuilders, befitting the long-standing association between them and Rolls-Royce.

WHAT IS A ROLLS-ROYCE?

*As one random encounter with an intriguing motorcar goes
to show, the question of what constitutes a Rolls-Royce is
not as clear cut as one might think*

WORDS AND PHOTOGRAPHY BY BILL WOLF

Last summer, I was in the process of reading several books by Joseph Conrad that examine, among other things, the concept of honor, when I did something that tarnished my own sense of integrity. This act may have been snide rather than corrupting, but my view of it is nevertheless similar to how Conrad's recurring character Charles Marlow feels about telling lies. "You know I hate, detest, and can't bear a lie, not because I am straighter than the rest of us, but simply because it appalls me," he says in *Heart of Darkness*. "There is a taint of death, a flavor of mortality in lies … what I want to forget. It makes me miserable and sick, like biting something rotten would do."

Something isn't right

It all started with me seeing a Rolls-Royce parked in front of a restaurant when I was driving through a small New Jersey town close to my home. It was obviously on display, a material advertisement for a limousine rental concern. A Silver Wraith maybe?

I drove back home to fetch my camera, returned, parked, and walked over to get a better look. Something didn't feel right. The car had recently been restored, but the leather had been replaced with material that was out of place in a Rolls-Royce, and the dash appeared too modern with its set of contemporary gauges, a small computer screen, and a large, metallic Rolls-Royce logo. The tires and hubcaps also lacked a vintage look, despite the prominent R-R in each center. And although the car had driving lamps from a Phantom and a genuine, if somewhat modified,

Rolls-Royce grille, it wasn't a Rolls-Royce at all —it was, in fact, an Austin Vanden Plas Princess!

The art of deception

I chatted up the owner, who was friendly and showed me his creation with a considerable amount of pride. Opening the custom hood latches, he revealed a gleaming Corvette engine that had been coupled to a GM400 transmission. The Princess also had a new suspension, while the hood had been lengthened and reshaped to fit the contours of the grille. This last had been crafted and fitted with great care and skill—much cleaner than even Bentley S to Silver Cloud conversions, which invariably leave an unsightly gap.

The tinted side windows were actually tinted glass, not merely plastic film; the front clip was from Fat Man; and in summer, the cabin would be well chilled through the Vintage Air installation. For those of you whose automotive tastes extend to hot rods and customs, as would be found in *Rod & Custom* magazine, Fat Man and Vintage Air will be familiar brands. In essence, then, this car wasn't even a Princess masquerading as a Rolls-Royce—it was a Princess masquerading as a custom. Or, perhaps more accurately, it was a customized Princess.

This is comparable to, say, the body of a 1958 Pontiac being mounted on a prefabricated chassis and fitted with contemporary brakes and suspension, a grille from a vintage Corvette, bucket seats from a much newer Pontiac, and a rebuilt, modified big-block Chevrolet engine. A car like that would be perfect for "cruisin' nights" or for display at a local hot-rod meet.

Previous pages: The unusual "Princess–Rolls-Royce" that got Bill thinking

Above: The car's iconic Rolls-Royce grille is genuine, and flawlessly fitted

Opposite, from top: Not the quality of dashboard one would expect of a Rolls-Royce; and one can see that the car's leathers lack the sumptuous feel of those associated with the marque

However, although this particular Princess might show up at such events, it would not be quite at home there. Nor would the car be welcome at a Rolls-Royce/Bentley rally, even if its outward appearance isn't actually unattractive.

Instead, this Princess was created for weddings or a fashionable night on the town. The rub, of course, is that the car was built on a deception, unsavorily using the Rolls-Royce logo and imitating the marque's design to cash in on its reputation. The owner of the Princess–Rolls-Royce (his term) assumed that most potential customers wouldn't realize that they weren't being chauffeured in an authentic Rolls-Royce and would enjoy the prestige and glamour as if they were. *Caveat emptor*?

Important differences

Which brings us to the question of what a Rolls-Royce actually is. Over the years, the marque has become so much more than a mere producer of automobiles. Today, its name is a concept, a benchmark of quality, elegance, prestige, and elan. In turn, this means that the problem with the car in question is a matter of degree.

As mentioned, its grille was perfectly mated to the hood, and the Vanden Plas body was not unattractive—in fact, I've seen less appealing coachwork on actual Rolls-Royces. However, the issue for the discerning eye arose from the Princess' interior. The leather, if genuine, looked cold and hard, nothing at all like the sumptuous Connolly leather that is found in many Rolls-Royce motorcars. In addition, the owner had pulled out the wood of the division for a more contemporary appearance, while the dashboard would be more suitable for a 1936 Ford hot rod—minus the R-R logos.

But my aesthetic evaluation of the car's interior begs the question: What if the cabin had been refashioned with finer fabrics and wood? What if it had been designed more elegantly, befitting the style and personality of a Silver Wraith—or, for that matter, a real Princess? And what if the chassis and drivetrain modifications had made it a much more powerful motorcar that was better to handle, more stable, and more comfortable than it actually is? Could it then, because of the revered and timeless grille, have been considered a modified, improved, and rebodied Rolls-Royce?

Defining a Rolls-Royce

The answer would, of course, be "No." One reason—surely the main one—for this negative reply is the patent absurdity of such a proposition. However, there's another reason, which points to a second aspect of the identity of Rolls-Royce automobiles: the chassis.

Throughout the coachbuilt era that ended with the last Silver Wraith and the last Phantom VI, the chassis (as well as the motor) was the car, with the grille as an identifying emblem. The coachwork, on the other hand, was, in a sense, merely a supplement to the engineering ideas and ideals that the chassis—the very soul of the marque—embodied.

"I'VE SEEN LESS APPEALING COACHWORK ON ACTUAL ROLLS-ROYCES"

Of course, the matter is actually a bit more complicated than that—not only because Rolls-Royce eventually started producing its own standard bodies, but also because the Company exerted great influence over coachbuilders, for instance, by withholding factory warranty for coachwork it deemed inappropriate. For those cars that were built using monocoque construction —from the Silver Shadow on through to the Silver Seraph—the idea that the chassis is the Rolls-Royce becomes even more problematic, an additional complication being that the Silver Seraph was fitted with a rebadged BMW engine. Another is the fact that, sad to say, Rolls-Royce was not without problems in quality control during this era. The problem with the load-leveling system of the Silver Shadow/Spirit series is but one example. I recall one journalist in, I believe, *Road & Track*, who suggested that the Silver Spur was not unlike a Lincoln with a fantastic interior. That is obviously a bit harsh, but like all such canards, there always remains a germ of truth.

Opposite: The Vanden Plas Austin
Princess, as advertised in 1956

"FOR THOSE FORTUNATE ENOUGH TO ACTUALLY USE THESE CARS, THERE
IS ALWAYS THAT SENSE OF EVERYTHING BEING EXACTLY AS IT SHOULD BE"

Elegance and engineering

The current series of Rolls-Royce automobiles offers an interesting twist because with the body now mounted on a space frame, it is conceivable that the concept of coachbuilding on a factory chassis could be reimagined. Also, as BMW now owns Rolls-Royce and designs and builds all new models, today's cars, though labeled "made in England," are essentially German. Does this, then, rule out the idea that Britishness is another defining feature of Rolls-Royce motorcars? My guess is that this is true for some, perhaps hardcore, aficionados.

So where does this leave us with regard to the question of the essence of a Rolls-Royce? Is it a combination of reputation, elegance, sound (if sometimes faulty) engineering, and pride? Tradition, lore, affirmation, and good taste are all part of the mix, while the driving experience of a Rolls-Royce must also be considered.

For those who are fortunate enough to actually use these cars on a regular basis, there is always that sense of everything being exactly as it should be. The driver experiences an organic feel of stability, power, assurance, and just the right balance of performance and luxury, while passengers and drivers alike know that to touch any control for any of the amenities is to experience meticulous accuracy, a study in proper and precise ergonomics. Plus, there is, after all,

Rolls-Royce's ineffability, the aura that surrounds each car, something that no other marque can quite match—and certainly something that no Princess poseur can even come close to achieving. It is this conclusion, I believe, that comes closest to answering my question.

Mea culpa

At the beginning I mentioned that something I did last summer has subsequently bothered me. Referencing Conrad might be somewhat of an affectation, but since my conscience is troubled I hope you will indulge me in a brief confession. Perhaps I am looking for atonement, or at least some comforting understanding.

As said, I chatted up the owner of the Princess, made inquiries as to the details of his car, and generally acted in a friendly way. The man himself was pleasant, proud, and friendly, too. That evening, I sent an email with images of this Princess–Rolls-Royce to some people who have an appreciation for Rolls-Royce motorcars. In it, I quoted lyrics from The Rolling Stones song "Start Me Up"—"It makes a grown man cry." On reflection, I found this unkind, snarky, and I was ashamed of the taint of snobbishness involved in this communication—"like biting something rotten." These reflections, then, are an attempt at expiation. Thank you for listening.

See the
Vanden Plas
AUSTIN
"PRINCESS"
(LIMOUSINE AND SALOON)
EXHIBITION

at the CarMart Ltd

SOLE LONDON AUSTIN DISTRIBUTORS

APRIL 16th —**APRIL 28th**

● Built by Craftsmen for those who insist on individuality and have a liking for luxury.
● One of the four Princess models will solve the problem of car selection for 1956 and many years to come.
● Prices from £2,686 7s. including tax. Trial Cars Available.

SHOWROOMS
STANHOPE HOUSE, 320, EUSTON ROAD, N.W.1.   EUSTON 1212
GLOUCESTER HOUSE, 150, PARK LANE, W.1.   GROSVENOR 3434
(CORNER OF PICCADILLY)

There's Prestige in Owning a "PRINCESS"

SPEEDING AHEAD

Kim Airey, Bentley Motor's Chief Operating Officer, considers the marque's racing heritage and looks forward to one of its biggest new ventures in years

How important is Bentley's legacy of racing excellence to the marque's current range?

KIM AIREY: With the Continental GT3 race car, we are very fortunate to create a motorsport story for fans of the brand today. Our return to the racing circuit last year was a celebration of our engineering prowess, as well as a nod to our storied history of epic races in the 1920s. We are continuing the tradition from which our company earned notoriety from its earliest days.

Our current motorsport endeavor is important in many ways. Our heritage has always been and will always be a part of who we are as a company and what goes into making our cars. By continuing the storyline from history we continue to deliver a message of performance and power. Our current owners and new fans alike are excited to share in this spirit. Driving and performance are two important elements of what one expects when behind the wheel of a Bentley. We bring the best of luxury and performance to the road.

How was the Mulsanne Speed received at the NAIAS? What makes it so special?

KA: The Mulsanne Speed received an overwhelming response from our customers and fans of the brand. It is our new flagship sedan. It offers assertive new styling combined with concealed technology and, naturally, endless customization options. Of course,

the Speed name signifies increased performance, but we have also brought improved efficiency with a 13 percent gain from a re-engineered, class-leading powertrain, which also increases the driving range. It is the pinnacle of performance and luxury—the ultimate expression of speed and style.

How does the Mulsanne Speed compare with the Continental GT Speed and Flying Spur? What does the current range say about Bentley?

KA: RROC members know that every Bentley is special. When our customers purchase a Bentley, it is a celebration of their success.

The Mulsanne Speed is the ultimate expression in our range and the pinnacle of our product offering. The ability to customize the Mulsanne is limitless. The iconic 6.75-liter motor propels the Mulsanne Speed to 60 mph in less than 5 seconds.

The Flying Spur is a true luxury and performance sedan. Its styling is contemporary, yet elegant and timeless. Let's not forget that the Flying Spur is the fastest, most powerful four-door Bentley ever, powered by our revered 6.0-liter 12 cylinder engine producing 616 hp capable of delivering a top speed of 200 mph.

The Continental GT is the ultimate Grand Tourer. With a top speed of 206 mph, the GT Speed's perfect blend of luxury and performance is clear from the moment you see

Opposite: Bentley Motors' new
Chief Operating Officer Kim Airey

the car. We have expanded the Continental GT line, offering customers more performance and styling options than ever before.

Why are bhp, top speed, and 0–60 mph acceleration so important at Bentley?
KA: Power, speed, and acceleration are certainly important, but they are only part of what makes a Bentley special. Delivering effortless performance is a crucial element for our customers. But so is the detail of craftsmanship.

> "OUR HERITAGE HAS ALWAYS
> BEEN A PART OF WHAT GOES
> INTO MAKING OUR CARS"

As they have for the better part of a century, our craftsmen and craftswomen continue to sculpt the leather and wood interiors by hand. Our designers and engineers bring the best of performance and luxury together, while maintaining comfort and refinement in every model we offer.

What is Bentley doing to expand into new markets? Which countries and regions is it targeting for future sales?
KA: The brand is in a very good position and continues to grow. We have continued to invest in new technologies and remain committed to bringing to market the best in luxury and performance. While 2014 was another record

"THE BENTAYGA WILL NOT SHIFT WHO WE ARE OR WHAT WE STAND FOR, BUT WILL PROVIDE A NEW ROAD ON THE BENTLEY JOURNEY"

year in our 96-year history, all markets face challenges over time that range from new legislation to economic factors. Because of this, it is important to always be prepared for the unexpected.

The Americas, China, and Europe, including the UK, continue to be key regions for the brand, but we are also seeing success in other markets, such as the Middle East and Asia Pacific, and will soon launch in Chile. The US continues to be the number-one market, accounting for 29 percent of global deliveries last year. But, to remain successful, we have to focus on all markets and continue to build luxury automobiles that not only meet customer demand but exceed expectations.

What can we expect from Bentley over the next 12 months? The Bentayga has to be one of the most eagerly anticipated models in the motoring diary—what does producing a luxury SUV mean for the evolution of Bentley?
KA: This is an important year and we have much to prepare for. With the roll-out of our new flagship sedan, the Mulsanne Speed; extensive updates across the Continental GT and Flying Spur families later this year; and of course the launch of the Bentayga, it will be a busy and exciting year ahead. Bentley now has the strongest model line-up ever, with a total of 13 models.

We are bringing Bentayga to market, quite simply, because our customers have asked for it. Every part of the business is preparing for this monumental launch. All new models must pass the test of being a true Bentley—that is, a passion for, and pursuit of, both luxury and performance. The Bentayga will arrive in the first half of 2016 and it will be true to the brand DNA of luxury, performance, quality, and craftsmanship. The model will create a new segment in the market for consumers looking for the pinnacle SUV, faster and more luxurious than any other. It will further expand Bentley's reach and engagement to new customers. It will not shift who we are or what we stand for, but will provide a new road to take customers on the Bentley journey.

Previous pages: The Mulsanne Speed more than lives up to its name

Opposite, from top: Bentley's skilled craftspeople work the cars' leather and wood interiors by hand to this day; the Continental GT Convertible delivers performance and luxury

BESPOKE BY NATURE

Rolls-Royce's Bespoke Design Team is continuing a legacy that dates back to Henry Royce's founding philosophy, as Eric C. Shepherd, President, Rolls-Royce Motor Cars NA, explains

The bespoke capabilities of Rolls-Royce hark back to the Company's origins; why is the personalizing of motorcars so integral to the marque's DNA?

ERIC C. SHEPHERD: Building a bespoke product goes back to the earliest days of Rolls-Royce and the philosophy of Sir Henry Royce himself. Royce set out to build the best cars in the world. His cars were designed for people who could afford the best of everything and knew precisely what they wanted. Bespoke is a natural extension of serving a very discerning market. He had a passion for building the best and realized that, while his cars would always be relatively few in number, they would carry a premium price. This model empowered him to design each motorcar to satisfy the specific taste of each individual owner. Borrowing from England's long heritage of custom clothiers, he adopted the word "bespoke."

In the years that followed, automobiles became more popular and most manufacturers aimed for high-volume products that called for standardized production. You might recall the phrase attributed to Henry Ford: "Any color you like, so long as it is black." While this philosophy brought affordable cars to the masses, Royce stuck with his vision of building the highest quality cars to the exacting standards of his limited universe of discerning owners. More than 110 years later, we are proud of the bespoke heritage he created. The objective of our modern Bespoke Design Team in Goodwood is to take individualization to never before seen levels using the historic legacy of British craftsmanship and the latest 21st-century technology. The result is limited only by the imagination of our owners.

What services does the Bespoke Design Team offer?

ECS: Paint colors and finishes are certainly one of the most popular bespoke options. After all, these are the easiest to envision and understand. We can create virtually any color imaginable. We can, and have, matched favorite lipsticks, nail polish, a favorite garment, or a sunset from a favorite painting or photo. We can make the finish glossy, matte, or anywhere in between. We can do coach lines, and any variety of hand-painted coats of arms, logos, and monograms, or even create an insignia. Naturally, we can do multiple body colors, divided as imagined by our owner, with the assistance of our bespoke team.

Interiors can also benefit from a wide range of bespoke choices. Again, we can match leather or fabric to virtually any color. If you want to make the interior of your Phantom match the interior of your Gulfstream 650, just provide our bespoke team with the design specs, or access to your plane, so that we can match it appropriately. It is a long-standing Rolls-Royce tradition to include coats of arms, initials, and other personal designs into our interiors as either inlays in the wood surfaces or embroidery on the seats and other interior panels. The most common choices for inlay materials include mother of pearl, silver or other precious metals, or gemstones. Our craftspeople can produce exquisite and highly detailed images using techniques from the ancient art of marquetry. One of the most exciting new bespoke designs we offer is a custom Starlight Headliner featuring more than one thousand LED lights laid out in the astronomical alignment from the day and location of your, or a loved one's, day of birth.

In 2014, we introduced several strikingly beautiful and compelling Bespoke Collections to help our owners imagine the creative capabilities of the Bespoke Team. Last year, these

Opposite: Rolls-Royce's latest bespoke collection—Nighthawk

Above: President of Rolls-Royce Motor Cars NA, Eric C. Shepherd

NIGHTHAWK
One of Nine

Above and opposite: Detailing from the Nighthawk Bespoke Collection, which features carbon-fiber dials, and Hotspur Red and Black leather seating

Following pages: Taking its lead from the design of stealth aircraft, Nighthawk exemplifies the Bespoke Design Team's ability to go from inspiring influences to beautifully crafted reality

included the Year of the Horse, Pinnacle Travel, Waterspeed, Metropolitan, Maharajah, and the Suhail Collection, with each demonstrating a unique blending of art, science, history, culture, technology, and imagination. These cars are absolutely fascinating and are destined to go down in history as unique examples of automotive art.

What are the most unusual bespoke options available?

ECS: That's hard to answer because one person's unusual request might be another's first thought. The beauty of bespoke is that it is not simply an option. Options are choices that one owner may specify and another may decline. Bespoke means something built especially for you—something that may never be requested again. That's the difference between bespoke and optional.

The bespoke ordering process is quite interesting, as well. It starts with a conversation between an owner and a sales consultant at one of our dealers. As they collaborate to specify a car, perhaps the owner brings up something they saw in a museum, a friend's plane, a boat, or some other inspiring environment. This item may not normally be something one thinks of as being part of a car, so the owner is not sure it is worth mentioning. Our Rolls-Royce sales consultants have learned over time that a quizzical look in an owner's eye might just be a challenge for our Bespoke Design Team.

Via emails and photos, phone calls, letters, or in some cases even personal visits, the Bespoke

Design Team acquires the information and images it needs to proceed. They work up a potential solution to satisfy the owner's desire. This can be as simple as a monogram for a coach line, or as complex as the installation of a dedicated communications system with oversize displays. Together, on a reiterative basis, they work out the unique design to the owner's satisfaction.

What was the thinking behind the recently launched Nighthawk Bespoke Collection? What are its most exciting features?

ECS: Nighthawk is a strikingly new interpretation of our dramatic Phantom Drophead Coupe. Inspired by the design of stealth aircraft, the collection features lustrous Diamond Black metallic paint against a Matt Diamond Black hood. The surface of its distinctive windscreen surround mimics the radar absorbent material used by the military.

The high-tech theme is carried through to the interior where carbon-fiber material mixes artfully with Hotspur Red and Black full-grain leather on the seats and other interior surfaces. Even the transmission tunnel and the boot, or trunk to us Americans, have been upholstered in leather. The instruments are also unique in the Nighthawk, featuring carbon-fiber dials and needles with incandescent orange tips. This is quite clearly not your father's Rolls-Royce and there will be just nine examples built in this exciting collection.

How large is the Bespoke Design Team and what are its areas of expertise?

ECS: The bespoke team is relatively small and elite; numbering just around ten, its members' specialty is being visionaries, artists, and designers. The actual fabrication is done by the craftsmen and craftswomen who work in the various shops of our Goodwood factory. The trick, if you will, of the bespoke

team is to take someone's inquiry or dream, and figure out how it might be turned into reality. The bespoke team creates renderings, design studies, and even models for customer revision and approval. When this happens, the approved design moves on to the appropriate production areas to be turned into a physical reality.

You might wonder how we acquire all of these highly talented craftspeople for our Goodwood facility. The answer is, we grow them! The South of England has a long history of training custom craftsman, and we've had a very aggressive apprenticeship program in operation for more than a decade now. As you might expect, the competition to get into the Rolls-Royce Motor Cars apprenticeship program is fierce, and it is a great honor to be accepted. This puts the company in the enviable position of being able to choose from the very best of the best. The program has been a huge success both for our company and for the talented young people who are looking to build a career.

Why does Bespoke appeal so much to Rolls-Royce owners?

ECS: The bottom line is that a Rolls-Royce owner wants something that only they have—a truly unique motorcar. There really is no other car company that can do bespoke to the same level as Rolls-Royce. You can purchase many fine luxury cars today that offer their customers nice options from a long punch list, but that is not the Rolls-Royce Motor Car way. In fact, in large cities, it is easy to come up to a major intersection and see a car just like yours coming at you from three other directions. When you make the magnitude of investment required to own a Rolls-Royce, you expect it to be a unique work of art. It is entirely

possible that in any given year we would not produce any two cars exactly the same.

Our owners take great pride in having exactly the car they want, built exactly the way they want it. And, it has always been so. When you submit an order for a new Rolls-Royce, your name joins a long list of some of the most creative, successful, powerful, and talented people to have lived in the past two centuries. People who fit that description want to have their achievements memorialized in their automobile.

What is next for the North American market and on the global stage?

ECS: By the time this interview is published, Rolls-Royce Motor Cars will have made at least two major announcements with global significance. While it would be inappropriate for me to discuss those at this moment, let me just say that we are a very healthy, successful, and profitable organization. We are very pleased that, since the introduction of the new Phantom in 2003, Rolls-Royce Motor Cars has indeed been reborn under the stewardship of BMW. The world, and particularly those people who really have a passion for this brand, recognize that we have been true to the belief system established by Sir Henry Royce well over a hundred years ago.

We're quite proud of our accomplishments, and I assure you that your members will be very impressed with the products and services we will be bringing to market in the years ahead. We believe that our greatest achievement has been to restore the Rolls-Royce name to its rightful position at the very top of the global automotive pyramid. Our ability to design and build truly bespoke products has been a critical factor in achieving this success.

Chapter 2
BON VOYAGE

PARADISE FOUND

As the only marina in Turkey with high-capacity mooring
for mega yachts, Palmarina Bodrum mixes an idyllic location
with superb amenities and technical services

"PALMARINA BODRUM HAS EVERYTHING YOU NEED, BUT IN ONE IDEAL LOCATION. IT'S THE KIND OF PLACE YOU DON'T WANT TO LEAVE"

resort attracts a select crowd throughout the year. Many celebrities, including supermodels Kate Moss and Naomi Campbell, are regularly sighted there; Bill Gates has been known to sail in discreetly, and *haut-monde* figures, such as Mick Jagger and Roman Abramovich, are thought to count it among their favorite destinations.

As Turkey's only high-capacity mooring for mega yachts, Palmarina Bodrum can house as many as eight vessels of up to 105 m in length. It also has an impressive capacity for 69 mega yachts of 40 m and over. And, for airborne visitors, the marina is easy to access thanks to a helipad on the roof of one of its restaurants, with a customs gate conveniently situated below.

Turkish diamond
"It's a wonderful place," says Cenk Bircan, Palmarina Bodrum's General Manager. "It has everything you need, but in one ideal location. Some people sail in, then stay for a couple of weeks or more—they never get bored. It's the kind of place you don't want to leave."

An impressive range of amenities provide plenty of reasons to stay. In addition to an open mall having 109 high-end shops and restaurants —including Nobu and Cipriani—there is an art gallery, a beach club, a spa, the luxurious night club Billionaire, and two hotels: Palmalife Marina Hotel and Palmarina Bodrum Boutique Hotel. Children can pass the time at Palmarina Bodrum's Kids' Paradise, which includes a water park, carousel, 7D cinema, and a mini zoo. The nearby city of Bodrum boasts a lively nightlife, and those interested in history can explore the Roman city of Ephesus, the Castle of Knights of St. John, and the ancient Mausoleum.

The marina has long had a green agenda, with banks of solar panels soaking up the copious sunshine for heating and power. And, although Palmarina Bodrum has an array of certifications, it is most proud to be the only marina in the

country to have been awarded the coveted ISO 9001: 2008 for quality management systems, issued by Lloyd's Register of Shipping.

Berth of the cool
Palmarina Bodrum is more than just a marina with a resort and an open mall. "We also provide extensive concierge services for our guests, and complete yacht services for their vessels," says Cenk. "Our technical facilities include a lift that can carry boats of up to 260 tons—or 45 m in length—and place them in dry dock. This way, repairs and maintenance on any scale can be carried out while owners pass the time in comfort."

Indeed, Palmarina Bodrum's affiliation with the service company Palyachting offers customers access to an extensive database of suppliers, technicians, and local professionals at all times. "Because of this, our guests find they have no need for any other agency because we supply everything," says Cenk. "It's a complete service." And for those seeking to buy, Palmarina Bodrum's extensive network can also connect them with yacht brokers, as well as owners.

"The mix of sunshine and seascapes might not be unique," says Cenk, "but the offering of a tranquil marina, endless amenities, a five-star concierge service, and ample provision of sights to see and activities to do is unrivaled." Everything you'd expect of a Turkish Riviera—and more. *www.palmarina.com.tr*

Often referred to as the Turkish Riviera, the Bodrum Peninsula—in the southwest of Turkey—enjoys a Mediterranean climate and sublime views of the turquoise Aegean Sea.

And, at the north-eastern tip of the peninsula sits the ancient sponge-fishing port of Yalikavak, home to the exclusive Palmarina Bodrum marina and resort. This international award-winning

POWER AND PASSION

Born of one man's desire to see his creation come to life, Massachusetts' Danalevi Corporation designs and develops eye-catching powerboats—notably its flagship Furina model

Once upon a time, a Massachusetts-based carpenter sketched the silhouette of a boat on a scrap of wood. His design combined the sleek style of vessels crafted in the 1930s and 1940s with the performance and strong curves of mid-century Cobras and Stingrays.

"I'd have been crazy to enter the boating industry with something unoriginal," says Ross Hartman, the carpenter-turned-designer behind boatmakers the Danalevi Corporation. "Instead, I started sketching a range of different boats that would blend the design elegance and finish of the past together with the convenience and power of modern technology."

"IF THE MIX OF POWER AND ELEGANCE DRAWS PEOPLE INITIALLY, IT'S THE THOUGHT-OUT DETAILS THAT RETAIN THEIR INTEREST"

During the design process of what would become the Furina model, Ross consulted naval architects and other boat-building professionals. As with a lot of creative endeavors, Ross's motivation is passion. "It's not uncommon for boat builders to lose their shirt in pursuing their passion," he says, "but it was important for me to do something I love—regardless of the risk."

Seaworthy and stylish

After 10 years of development, Ross's company Danalevi made its first prototype—and Furina was born. Seeing what had been only an idea turn into a design that was both seaworthy and stylish was a dream come true for him. "It was incredibly surreal to see something that formed in my head come to life on the water," he says. "It made all the hard work completely worth it."

Whenever Furina is in the public eye, either cruising on the lake or making the rounds at boat shows, Ross is gratified by the public response. "People absolutely adore the boat when they see it," he says. "They congratulate me on bringing something new and innovative to the market. Boaters are particularly impressed —they tell me that Furina's unique design is a breath of fresh air."

Because Furina is aimed at recreational boaters, ease of use is incredibly important.

"People want boats that are more like cars, in that you can just get in them, turn the key and go," says Ross. "So we made this ease a priority when we designed the cockpit, and included new technologies."

Fully customizable

To bump up the luxury factor, Danalevi has purposely designed its production process to allow the boats to be as customizable as possible. "The Furina is definitely not a cookie-cutter design," says Ross. "She is a truly bespoke powerboat." Indeed, as well as being able to choose the engine size and the color of the boat, customers can customize details such as the interior finish and decking.

If the novel mix of power and elegance is what draws people initially, it is the carefully thought-out details that retain their interest. With a Volvo Penta 380 hp engine giving the boat a top speed of 60 mph, and a well-designed interior that ensures a comfortable ride, Furina is a luxury runabout.

This is just the beginning of the journey for Danalevi. Ross's future plans for his company's product line include a sport catamaran, a 32-ft powerboat, and an open-bow model.

But even that isn't the end of this fairy-tale. Ross explains: "My passion for designing powerboats that people gravitate towards and appreciate is never-ending."
www.danalevi.com

"THE LEVEL OF INSIDER ACCESS
WE OFFER MEANS THAT EACH
PERSONALIZED ITINERARY MAKES
THE MOST OF ANY DESTINATION"

TOURS DE FORCE

With more than 30 years of experience providing bespoke travel packages to India, family-owned tour company Greaves Tours is spreading its wings

Ian Cambata claims that: "We could take you to India a dozen times and each trip would be completely different. It wouldn't feel as if you were in the same country." Coming from the Vice President of Greaves Tours, the boast is entirely justified. For more than 30 years, this third-generation, family-owned tour company has designed luxury holidays to India, with special experiences in every trip.

The family's extensive roots and business connections in India furnishes Greaves with unrivaled insider access and first-hand knowledge of the country's celebrated sights and hidden gems. This is heightened by the firm's unparalleled access to and history with private aircraft in the region. And working with industry-leading partners, like Oberoi Hotels & Resorts—whose Oberoi Udaivilas resort in Udaipur (pictured left) is a prime example—provides clients with world-renowned service and luxury amenities across India.

Greaves Tours significantly expanded its portfolio in 2014, and now includes such unique global adventures as gorilla-spotting in Rwanda, seats at the Monaco Grand Prix, and taking gastronomic tours of Argentina.

A passion for travel

The Greaves Tours story began with the Cambata family's unquenchable passion for travel—one that continues to drive the company to this day. "Most of my family is involved in the company," says Ian. "We are very fortunate to be able to work together on a shared passion, with destinations we love." Ian and his family themselves regularly host tours, liaising—via the Greaves office in India—with a network of guides that includes local artists, personal shoppers, and academics. In the North Indian city of Varanasi, for example, a dean of one of its schools can accompany clients to provide an in-depth view on the city's culture and religion.

Family connections also enable Greaves to host society dinners in Mumbai, at which clients can meet Bollywood stars and members of Indian society. And when *Departures* magazine celebrated its 25th birthday, Greaves arranged a gala dinner with the Maharaja of Jodhpur in the Mehrangarh Fort. The company also caters to the other end of the scale. "My parents recently led a hiking group through Bhutan, a newer destination for us, which involved camping outdoors with a shower tent," says Ian. "It's about giving the client the experience they are looking for, whatever that may be."

Tailor-made tours

Around 98 percent of itineraries are bespoke, although there are also 73 established tours that clients are able to choose from. "Most of our business comes from word of mouth or personal referrals," says Ian. "We are known for our high-touch, high-quality tours. We can create something very intimate and exclusive for our clients, and that is why they keep coming back!"

And with the launch of the new tour portfolio in 2014, the concept of "tailor-made travel" now extends far beyond India—operating in Africa, Asia, Europe, and the Americas. "We asked ourselves: how do we enhance a destination?" says Ian. "With Myanmar, for example, this might involve a private hot air balloon rising above the temple-studded plains of Bagan, providing a unique perspective and a lasting memory of an amazing country. That kind of special touch is what we aim to provide."

Greaves Tours' standout reputation is based on the experience and positive feedback of generations of passionate, curious travelers. "The real luxury these days is having the time to travel," says Ian. "The level of insider access we offer means that each personalized itinerary makes the most of time in any destination."
www.greavesindia.com

VOYAGE OF DISCOVERY

Ker & Downey creates inspirational and unique luxury holidays to a host of exotic international destinations, custom-made for a discerning clientele

Ker & Downey earned its name in luxury travel by taking the path less traveled, escorting clients on inspiring, experiential journeys and introducing them to people and cultures at an intimate level that few others offer.

"It isn't always about doing the flashiest thing," says Vice President David Jones. "Clients receive an experience that is unique to them because we have taken the time to learn about what wine, music, or art they like; what sport or adventure activities they enjoy; which books interest them."

The company has an incomparable ability to connect people and places, an ability achieved through its international network of experts and a Texas-based team of seasoned travelers with first-hand knowledge of their recommended destinations. Ker & Downey curates dozens of itineraries, varying from golf or culinary journeys, to family trips and safaris. Around 90 percent of clients then customize their travel plans around their passions and interests.

A global reach

Ker & Downey operates in 83 countries, each offering new discoveries. Itineraries are designed by experts who, in tandem with on-location teams, construct creative, bespoke plans.

One of the ways the company accomplishes this is through providing exclusive access, which is a cornerstone of its philosophy. For instance, a family traveled with Ker & Downey to Paris one Christmas. Knowing the son's love for medieval armor, the company arranged

a surprise private viewing of an armor collection in a French chateau on Christmas Day.

Indeed, no task is too daunting and no locale too obscure. Take, for example, the clients who wished to fly by helicopter into the remote reaches of Papua New Guinea. Ker & Downey executed their wishes effortlessly, and the couple was greeted with a generous welcome by local tribespeople who had only witnessed a few Westerners in their lifetime. This kind of offering is crucial for an authentic experience. "If you don't encounter real people, all you come back with are photos," says David.

To ensure that such tours go without a hitch, members of staff review each itinerary at least five times, enhancing them with extra flourishes—such as hotel transfers in white Jaguars—where needed.

A history of excellence

Ker & Downey is, in particular, able to deliver unrivaled experiences for travelers drawn to the allure of Africa. Given that wildlife is usually the first item on every client's Africa bucket list, the company focuses its attention on the 10-plus countries known for their unique flora and fauna. Ker & Downey also excels in journeys for multi-generational families, melding such activities as zip-lining, river rafting, whale watching, and shark diving. "An African safari is an experience where you can fully escape," says David. "A family can be a family without the distractions of everyday life."

> "CLIENTS RECEIVE AN EXPERIENCE UNIQUE TO THEM BECAUSE WE HAVE TAKEN THE TIME TO LEARN ABOUT WHAT THEY ENJOY"

The teams who arrange such memorable trips are equally committed to the company's philanthropic work, lauded in 2014 by PURE Life Experiences in London. President and CEO David Marek personally helps to distribute 15,000 mosquito nets to outlying villages in Uganda each year, and Ker & Downey frequently sponsors Ugandan medical students and doctors. The company also helped fund a rhino repatriation project in Botswana.

Ker & Downey's sophisticated—and often, as David puts it, quirky—clients get more than a luxury journey when they book. The painstaking detail that goes into every itinerary means clients experience a destination in an entirely new way— making the path less traveled ever more appealing.
www.kerdowney.com

FIVE-STAR TREATMENT

Located in coastal Georgia, Sea Island resort has been
providing its guests with unparalleled levels of quality
and personal service since 1928

For the private, five-star resort Sea Island, it's all about the personal touch. "Whether it's providing 24-hour butler service at The Lodge or recognizing returning guests, personal service is paramount," says Scott Steilen, Sea Island's President.

At this exclusive family-friendly resort, staff go above and beyond what is expected of them to ensure a quality experience for guests who have included presidents and film stars. This tradition of service and "gracious hospitality" was started by Bill Jones and automobile magnate Howard Coffin when they founded their "friendly little hotel" here in 1928—and it continues to this day.

It goes to explain why Sea Island is the only resort in the world to have earned coveted Forbes Five-Star ratings in no fewer than four categories for the past seven years in a row. These awards reflect the unparalleled quality and service delivered at The Cloister, a Mediterranean-style retreat, and at The Lodge at Sea Island Golf Club, which boasts impressive ocean and golf course views.

Highly rated

It is not only Sea Island's accommodations that have been honored, but also the dining and spa experiences it provides guests. The Georgian Room restaurant—where guests are served on hand-painted china—and the 23-treatment room spa are five-star holders. To earn such a rating, there are hundreds of standards that need to be met. According to Scott, it is the lengths that staff go to for guests that sets Sea Island apart from the competition.

"One example," he says, "was when a guest, a young lady, wanted to ride a horse, but the experience didn't go as she'd hoped. Staff bought a stuffed horse and presented it to her with a note of apology from the horse, asking her to return for another try. She did, it went well, and the little girl was very happy.

It shows how the quality of our guests' experience is so important to us."

Home on the range

Away from the first-class accommodations, dining and pampering, Sea Island is the place for golf enthusiasts. There are three 18-hole championship courses, including the Seaside Course, which is home to the PGA TOUR's McGladrey Classic and affords golfers a links-style golf experience.

> "GOLFING GUESTS MAY FIND THEMSELVES STANDING NEXT TO PROS ON THE DRIVING RANGE"

The resort's Golf Performance Center teaches all skill levels and has more top-50 instructors than any other teaching facility. More than 10 touring professionals—including Matt Kuchar and Zach Johnson—not only train there but also choose to live there. "It means that golfing guests may find themselves standing next to pros on the driving range," says Scott.

Sporting pursuits abound in addition to golf, including hunting, tennis, squash, and nature experiences. Sea Island also hosts themed weekends; on one of these, *Downton Abbey* enthusiasts got to meet several of the show's stars, as well as Jessica Fellowes, author of the series' official companion books.

Sea Island offers activities to suit every taste, where guests of all ages are encouraged to explore its five miles of private beach and engage in a variety of water sports including kayaking, sailing and the very popular stand-up paddleboarding.

The secret of Sea Island is that it offers five-star facilities while always remaining a "friendly little hotel" at heart, a place where staff go the extra mile to ensure that everyone has a memorable stay.

www.seaisland.com

SMOOTH SAILING

As the founder of yacht acquisition firm Boston Yacht Consulting, Ron Housman's love of a life on water is one that he relishes sharing with his clients

Ever since first steering his grandfather's 1963 Hatteras motor yacht at the age of nine, Ron Housman has devoted himself to a life on water. For the past 26 years, the Boston-based broker has lived on motor yachts year-round, giving him a considerable edge over the heavy competition within the yacht brokerage business.

"Because I live on a yacht, I understand what makes a yacht livable and conducive to spending more time on board," says Ron. "I've been on 100-footers that feel like 70-footers, and 100-footers that feel like 130-footers—it's all about layout and the ergonomics of the design."

Ron is a USCG-licensed captain for vessels up to 100 tons. His current home is a luxurious Hatteras motor yacht, which allows for long summers on Martha's Vineyard and Nantucket. When recommending yachts for upscale clients —from sports stars and entertainers, to diplomats and businesspeople—he understands the world in which they operate.

An eye for craftsmanship

Before he launched Boston Yacht Consulting, Ron had his own custom furniture business for 25 years, designing high-end bespoke furniture and antique reproductions. This understanding of construction and craftsmanship makes him particularly skilled at vetting the quality of a yacht build and enables him to easily explain to clients exactly what they're getting for their money.

His commitment to red-carpet service extends to all aspects of his company, whether it's finding a client the highest-quality vessel to suit their lifestyle, or helping those who dream of building their own luxury yacht. As an affiliate of United Yacht Sales, the country's largest yacht brokerage, Ron can access inside knowledge from a collegial network of professionals. But it's the ongoing support that he offers beyond the sale that has enabled Ron to build and retain a loyal customer base. "I'm always available by phone, 24/7, to answer any question or take care of any problem that a client may have," he says. "It's as simple as that."

Specializing in vessels from $500,000 to $100 million and beyond, Boston Yacht Consulting has the flexibility and authority to negotiate the best possible deals for its clients. A comprehensive consultation ensures the right fit and, as an instrument-rated private pilot with his own plane, Ron is able to fly his clients to inspect yachts all along the Eastern Seaboard.

A significant number of Ron's clients are first-time yacht buyers and he's passionate about sharing the calming powers of life at sea with them. "Being on the water, spending time on the water—it's good for the soul," says Ron. "I want people to experience that for themselves."

www.bostonyachtconsulting.com

FLIGHTS OF FANCY

With an impressive fleet of luxury, large-cabin aircraft and some of the world's most experienced pilots, Jet Edge International is bringing style to the skies

As one who dreamed of a life working in the movies, Bill Papariella makes for an unlikely aviation high-flyer. But, after working as a senior producer at Universal Studios, he moved into aviation and found that the two industries were not dissimilar. Both benefit from an entrepreneurial spirit, the ability to get things done, and a talent for getting people where they need to be.

Such qualities have been key to the success of Jet Edge International. Since Bill bought the company in 2012 with a fleet of just six aircraft, it has grown to become a leader in large-cabin private aviation, boasting 40 luxury Gulfstream, Dassault, and Bombardier jet types. The company now has bases in California, New York, Florida, Colorado, Nevada, Georgia, Tokyo, and Hong Kong, and its jets fly all over the world.

"We manage a billion dollars' worth of aircraft," says Bill, the company's President and CEO. "Working with both individuals and corporations, we offer a complete range of aircraft services. These range from full charter management and crew management to flight operations and a maintenance facility."

A touch of luxury

In late 2014, Jet Edge added a third Gulfstream G650 to its fleet—a $65 million aircraft that's the most impressive in its line-up. It's one of the most technologically advanced business jets available, with the ability to fly non-stop for more than 8,000 miles and reach speeds of 705 mph or mach 0.925—almost the speed of sound.

Speed and range are just two attributes of the G650 that the discerning business traveler will appreciate. Inside, it has the tallest, longest, and widest cabin in its class, international Wi-Fi, and an iPhone app to control several TV screens and shades. The cabin can also be pressurized to a very high level: even when flying at 50,000 ft, it can feel like a 3,000 ft flight, leaving passengers far less tired and much more comfortable.

Naturally, safety is paramount at Jet Edge. The company has an impeccable record, receiving a platinum rating for safety from the Aviation Research Group—the group's highest level of recognition. This is largely due to its pilots, who each have more than 12,000 flight hours of experience, well in excess of the Federal Aviation Administration's requirement of 1,500 hours for commercial pilots. In addition, Jet Edge pilots attend professional training courses twice a year.

The company's clients range from industry moguls to global innovators. Whoever they are, Jet Edge's dedicated team of 78 oversees every aspect of their trip, customized to their precise needs.

Success aside, with one of Jet Edge's Gulfstream IVs gracing the cover of *Vogue*'s April 2014 issue, the company is clearly also capturing the glamour of private air travel —which is good news for dreamers like Bill. *www.flyjetedge.com*

Chapter 3
GRAND DESIGNS

OUTSIDE THE BOX

The inventive work of New York design and architecture firm 212box has attracted a global portfolio of clients that includes Kilian and Christian Louboutin

The name of Eric Clough and Eun Sun Chun's architectural design firm—212box—might be something of a misnomer. Though the numbers refer to the telephone area code for Manhattan, where Eric and Eun are based, it's impossible to place these multidisciplinary designers into any kind of box.

The firm's breadth of offering is vast. It undertakes high-end residential, commercial, and retail work, as well as managing four other departments: graphics, products, film, and animation.

"EVERY PROJECT IS AN INVENTION AND A CHANCE FOR US TO INNOVATE"

There is, however, one factor that unifies all of 212box's architectural work. "Each of our holistic designs makes use of a strong narrative that ties every medium together," says Eric, "whether that narrative be based on cultural inspiration, steeped in history, or personal to the individual client."

Store stories
Narrative-led design is evident in some of the firm's most high-profile work, notably for the shoe designer Christian Louboutin. The 212box team has designed almost every Louboutin store across the globe, with each design heavily influenced by its particular location.

"Our team travels and researches the culture, craftsmanship, and local trades of the area,"

says Eun, "in view of bringing something of the locality to the store." Thus, the Mumbai store features locally hand-carved wooden tiles that undulate along the walls, whereas embossed and pleated leather—as well as embroidery work—feature heavily in the Louboutin men's store in Paris.

Indeed, this kind of collaborative working goes to the heart of 212box. The firm uses fabricators, different trades, and artisans, depending on the particular needs of a client. Its work can be seen all over the world, including the creation of a geometric, cloud-like ceiling in Harrods' Shoe Heaven for Louboutin, Kilian's new flagship store in Paris, and a spectacular camouflage wall with six-inch spikes in Dubai.

However, not all projects are land-based and the firm has also renovated the interior of two private jets and a 105 ft yacht.

Manhattan mystery
Thoughtful design also translates to the firm's residential work. One particular project for an apartment on the Upper East Side of Manhattan—titled the "Mystery on Fifth Avenue" apartment—attracted the attention of *The New York Times* and London's *Financial Times* after its completion in 2008. Motivated by a desire to inspire the four children in the family, 212box incorporated a *Da Vinci Code*-style narrative into the design. The result was a whole series of magical clues, ciphers, and code-breaking games to point to the hiding places of various creations.

"We may have got a little carried away with it," says Eric. "We created all of the puzzles and ciphers ourselves, as well as composing an entire original CD of music and a 230-page novel to accompany the apartment. In total, we collaborated with more than 40 artisans, on top of gutting and renovating the entire apartment. It was fun, but also a real exploration and affirmation of our capabilities."

And this is just one of many mold-breaking designs that 212box has developed. "Every project is an invention and a chance for us to innovate," says Eric. "Our many disciplines help to empower our work and our thinking." Thinking, indeed, that is miles out of the box.
www.212box.com

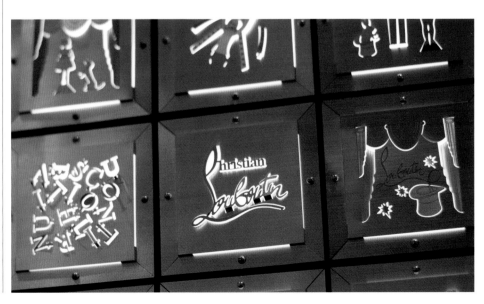

BUILT EXPRESSION

Manhattan design firm Andre Tchelistcheff Architects is adding a global outlook to the classic principles of structure, function, and beauty

With each new architectural endeavor, Andre Tchelistcheff asks himself two questions: what is the essential nature of the place, and how can he and his colleagues, as architects and designers, transform that quality to its fullest and most beautiful expression?

"We work closely with our clients to develop elegant and resonant design solutions," says Andre, director of Andre Tchelistcheff Architects. "Successful design strives to be harmonious with the locale and the ideals of the client. It takes into careful consideration a myriad of issues: the historical, environmental, and financial parameters of a project in relation to its aesthetic impact."

Andre's practice, based in SoHo, New York City, was founded in 1998 and has since gone on to complete a host of award-winning projects for high-profile clients in both the USA and abroad. With commissions in New York City, California, Connecticut, Utah, Russia, and the Bahamas, the design firm has established itself as capable of delivering a bespoke experience to its clientele across diverse locations.

A global perspective
Andre was born in San Francisco to Russian émigrés and then raised in the Middle East and Southeast Asia. He received a B.A. in Architecture from the University of California, Berkeley, and a Master of Architecture from Massachusetts Institute of Technology. His graduate research projects with the Aga Khan Foundation took him to the Soviet Republic of Tatarstan, and the Yemeni capital, Sana'a.

This international background enables Andre to fully appreciate and respect the extent to which design and architecture informs life experiences, whether working with historic structures, rural vernacular, or sophisticated contemporary cosmopolitan living.

In keeping with Andre's background and beliefs, his company's work reflects the diversity and complexity of his various travels and studies. Recent projects range from a sleek, modernist, highly polished renovation for a duplex apartment on Park Avenue with a custom floating staircase, to a carefully crafted wood and bronze sauna building for an estate overlooking the Hudson River. There are also significant historic restorations: the Cartier Mansion in Manhattan, an 18,000-sq ft Beaux Arts townhouse built in 1916; the transformation of a 19th-century apartment building into a private residence in Moscow, Russia; and the Villa Maria, a 21,000-sq ft Jazz Age estate in the Hamptons, Long Island.

Stylistic diversity
The firm's associates hail from an array of international backgrounds, and have a deep appreciation and knowledge of the variation possible in architectural expression. However, they are unified by a commitment to producing works of the highest quality. "With each project, we seek an understanding between both the structural clarity of the building and its emotive potential," says Andre. "The social, economic, and pragmatic elements —such as material selection and construction techniques—are analyzed to produce the most coherent expression of the project's aspirations."

> "SUCCESSFUL DESIGN STRIVES TO BE HARMONIOUS WITH THE LOCALE AND THE IDEALS OF THE CLIENT"

The firm has been honored with numerous design awards, such as the 2014 Stanford White Award for Historic Preservation from the Institute of Classical Architecture, and has had work published in esteemed publications including *Architectural Digest*, *NY Cottage & Garden*, and *The New York Times*, as well as the book *Engaging with the Classics: Collection of New Traditional Residential Masterworks*.

"Successful design and architecture," says Andre, "should provide an enduring affirmation of the human spirit, whether in the smallest of details or in the grandest of gestures." It is the manifestation of that spirit that truly distinguishes the work of this extraordinary firm.
www.tchelistcheff.com

FIRM FOUNDATIONS

Focusing on craftsmanship, integrity, and impeccable service, premier builder and construction manager D. Reis Contracting Corp. of New York raises the bar for the best of the best

Aman's home is his castle, as the saying goes—and no one respects the pride and personal investment that people put into their residences more than Edward Reis, Principal of the New York-based premier builder, D. Reis Contracting Corp.

"Our core business is commissioned private residences in Manhattan and the surrounding areas, working with high-end, discerning clients," says Edward. Expectations of the firm are high, but D. Reis knows how to deliver, thanks to its breadth of expertise, understanding of structural complexities and quality finishes, and levels of integrity and reliability.

"Our teams have a very thoughtful and diligent approach to our projects," says Edward, "as they develop, during construction, and for ongoing maintenance. We are very attentive to every detail, including how a space will be lived in and properly cared for in the future. We take a lot of pride in our work because it's not just our business but our family legacy."

A family legacy

That legacy dates back a generation. Edward's father, Domingos, was born into a small farming community in Portugal during a difficult recession. Aged 22, he traveled to the US, pursuing his passion to work as a high-end cabinet-maker, and studied English and interior design. By 1977, "Dominick"—now 27 years old—had acquired a degree and secured the capital to start a small woodworking shop, D. Reis Furniture Corp. This became one of the region's most highly sought-after and well-respected luxury millwork companies. And, with his history in construction, Dominick soon added the sister company, D. Reis Contracting Corp., to his portfolio.

Edward has headed up D. Reis since 2008. He was brought up in the business and worked his way up through various roles in the field and management to a position of leadership as CEO. "Growing up, I worked summers in the shop and field," he says, "and later attended college for business before focusing on a BA from the fine arts program with a concentration on interior design." His sister, Yvonne, studied accounting and went on to become a Certified Public Accountant with one of the big six account firms at the time before moving on to Robinson Lerer & Montgomery and later becoming Director of Finance for Saatchi & Saatchi Wellness—part of Publicis Groupe, one of the big four agency firms. Yvonne joined D. Reis in 2009 as its Chief Financial Officer.

A personal matter

Employing approximately 85 people across its contracting and furniture companies, D. Reis prides itself on providing the personal touch.

"I know everyone that works for me, and our clients get a lot of attention from me personally," says Edward. "We take on a limited number of projects each year to ensure we can offer a higher level of service. We're about building long-term relationships. We work hard to be very attentive listeners and anticipate potential issues."

The company's breadth of construction expertise in the high-end market is among the most well rounded in the New York area—and the culture of D. Reis continues to attract some of the finest talent. Yvonne and Edward are dedicated to establishing collaborative working relationships with architects and owners from the very early stages. They also continue that relationship in the following years as part of ongoing maintenance programs.

It's a philosophy that has served D. Reis well, building the company's reputation and reach, and ensuring that each client's home is, always, his castle.

www.dreiscontracting.com

"WE TAKE A LOT OF PRIDE IN OUR WORK BECAUSE THIS IS NOT JUST OUR BUSINESS, IT'S OUR FAMILY LEGACY"

PRIDE OF PLACE

New York-based D'Alessio Inspired Architectural Designs
works closely with its clients in order to fully understand,
and then exceed, their expectations

When it comes to building the perfect home, everyone has different needs and desires, which is why the President of D'Alessio Inspired Architectural Designs is committed to taking a hands-on approach to every project. Founder Andrea D'Alessio Jr. is renowned for forging such close relationships with his clients that he is able to interpret and realize their vision beyond even their own expectations. His exquisite, award-winning creations are true legacy homes, designed to stand the test of time.

Charlé-John Cafiero, Marketing Director for the New York-based company, explains that trust is paramount in successfully designing and constructing the castles, luxury mansions, and European châteaux on which D'Alessio works.

"Andrea's attitude is that, if he doesn't develop a relationship, then clients can't trust him to spend huge amounts of their money," says Charlé-John. "They need to be able to trust why he's doing it a certain way. And he has to have that trust to give them what they want."

Inspiring confidence

Andrea's impeccable credentials and personal involvement with every stage of the process inspire confidence. He worked for many years as a stonemason before starting his own business and has an encyclopedic knowledge of 18th- and 19th-century classical design, in which the company specializes. He visits every proposed site himself, making several detailed sketches that he revises with clients before creating a final set of conceptual design renderings.

By working so closely with each client, Andrea ensures that he has captured the essence of their unique vision, before enhancing it with his own creativity and experience. His passion for craftsmanship and his meticulous attention to detail—combined with state-of-the-art building technology—means that D'Alessio is leading the way in creating timeless luxury homes.

"It's the creative detail that clients come to us for," says Charlé-John. "The architectural details are what give a home that luxury feeling and that sense of warmth."

All in the detail

Examples of this creative detail include a herringbone pattern pool surround that Andrea designed using travertine, a form of limestone. "Everything was hand-cut in one-inch blocks and then individually placed," says Charlé-John.

"Andrea created that pattern on site and showed his stone people how to do it, getting down on his hands and knees to do it with them."

That particular project won an International Property Award for Residential Landscape Architecture, one of a number of prestigious accolades the company has earned over the years.

"THE ARCHITECTURAL DETAILS ARE WHAT GIVE A HOME THAT LUXURY FEELING AND THAT SENSE OF WARMTH"

Another ongoing project involves gutting and restoring an 18,000 sq ft Elizabethan-influenced, English Cotswold-style manor house dating back to 1929 on New York's Long Island Gold Coast. Charlé-John describes how the painstaking process has included inviting several experts to inspect the building's "gorgeous" but unpractical leaded windows, to consider how they can be maintained and made fit for 21st-century living. "That's the kind of client that we're working with," he says. "People who really care about their properties."

Their devotion to getting every single last detail right is matched only by Andrea's, who is passionate about working closely with each client to interpret their vision and then drawing on his own creative ability to take it even further. The houses he designs are not only architecturally outstanding but—with every detail created in close collaboration with the owners—they truly are legacy homes to be passed down through the generations.

www.builtbydalessio.com

UNIQUE BY DESIGN

Whether for a distinguished home or a luxury hotel,
Los Angeles-based Darrell Schmitt Design Associates
creates individual interiors for individual clients

Darrell Schmitt's mission in life is to provide inspiring creative solutions to interior design problems. His award-winning Los Angeles practice—Darrell Schmitt Design Associates, Inc (DSDA)—creates bespoke designs for residential and corporate clients across the US, and his hospitality designs have received acclaim around the world. Together with his team, Darrell draws upon four decades' worth of experience in contemporary design to create workable, beautiful, and comfortable interiors.

"I see each new project as a problem to be solved," says Darrell. "Often, clients may not initially have a clear concept of how they'd like an interior to look. They may not fully envision what they want, so our job is to interpret and read between the lines to expand upon the expression of each individual client's wishes, and to bring harmony to the way they live."

A bespoke vision

Rather than promoting any signature style, DSDA's finished interiors take their form through interaction with each client. Darrell and his team conduct extensive interviews with each client to learn more about his or her personality and to find out what they need from their interior. DSDA endeavors to ensure that each project has a fresh look and attitude from the start, and that each completed interior is unique.

The firm has a core team of experienced designers, but also enlists other qualified specialists and artisans depending on the scale of the project. Recent large projects have ranged from major Southern California hotels and resorts, to the design of a strikingly modern interior for a grand residence in Saudi Arabia.

"Clients' tastes have changed greatly over the past few years," says Darrell. "I'm finding that more people are seeking innovative, contemporary designs. Huge strides in lighting mean that new LED schemes can transform modern living, and a plethora of new materials and products help to create dramatic solutions for interior spaces."

"CLIENTS' TASTES HAVE CHANGED OVER THE PAST FEW YEARS. I'M FINDING THAT MORE PEOPLE ARE SEEKING INNOVATIVE, CONTEMPORARY DESIGNS"

Darrell is a Fellow of the American Society of Interior Designers. His design vocabulary draws on a thorough knowledge of classical architecture, as well as more contemporary sources. "We're very comfortable working with architects," he says. "We are routinely involved with them on new-build projects from conception, and often work in different locations around the world."

Reworking the classics

One recent residential assignment was the major regeneration of a 180-year-old London townhouse. "The 35,000 sq ft space presented an interesting design proposition," says Darrell. "A building with protected heritage status brings with it challenges for any designer." DSDA's end result managed to maintain the existing classic Regency detailing, while sensitively adding contemporary furnishings and art.

"Inspiration always comes from our clients and the spaces we are working with," says Darrell. "Each client's desire, coupled with architectural opportunities, lead us to places we never expected to go with our designs, and that's why each project is unique."

Intelligent designs have earned DSDA ecological awards, including LEED (Leadership in Energy and Environmental Design) Platinum Certification from the US Green Building Council. This certification acknowledges the company's dedication to using sustainable materials in a California beach house project, whose elegant plaster and glass exterior works seamlessly with subtle interiors to cleverly integrate the project's commitment to energy efficiency.

Darrell Schmitt Design Associates' designs strive to bring harmony into the lives of its clients. By creating spaces that are both personal and luxurious, it proves that interiors can be efficient, beautiful and—of course—practical.

www.darrellschmittdesignassociates.com

TRUE TO FORM

Fresh, timeless designs and a meticulous attention to detail have earned Los Angeles-based design company FORM a devoted clientele and a growing portfolio of beautiful, innovative spaces

Compelled by a passion for beauty and a deep understanding of function, design company FORM is headed by duo Joshua Rose and Rafael Kalichstein. Inspired by the notion of seamless, flawless design, the duo's work fuses form and function into one harmonious entity. "It's a holistic relationship," says Joshua, "through which we are able to bring exquisite, imaginative, artistic solutions to the use of space."

FORM's high-end portfolio of private, commercial, and hospitality commissions, which range in location from Beverly Hills to Manhattan, is proof of Joshua and Rafael's passion and their keen sensitivity to each individual client.

Thoughtful approach

The Los Angeles-based design partnership believes that interiors should be welcoming, sustainable, and sensitive to their context. "Spaces speak, so for a design to be successful the designer has to listen," says Rafael. "Context is a huge consideration. The grounds, views, and age of a property all influence its 'voice,' as does a client's character and lifestyle."

Though the firm works across genres, FORM's designs are consistently both chic and timeless. The firm's approach is heavily influenced by the words of architect and designer Carlo Mollino: "Everything is permissible as long as it is fantastic." Joshua adds: "Whether it manifests as a priceless antique or a repurposed piece of driftwood, nothing is too precious or too odd to be considered, provided its form and function enhance the space."

With projects ranging from a single room to new builds, FORM boasts a roster of discerning clients. "We offer a truly bespoke experience," says Rafael. "We care to get to know the people with whom we work and the way they want to live. We are tireless in pursuing the fulfillment of our clients' needs.

"WE ARE COMMITTED TO THE IDEA THAT LIVING WITH BEAUTY ELEVATES THE HUMAN EXPERIENCE. IT CAN TRULY TRANSFORM A PERSON'S LIFE"

It's a symbiotic relationship in which collaboration and consideration are mutual."

Perhaps because of this attuned approach, FORM enjoys a high client return rate. "With one individual, we are working on a sixth project," says Joshua. "We are committed to the idea that living with beauty elevates the human experience and that we have the transformative power to change a person's life through enhancing his or her environment. Nevertheless, it is a commitment rooted in the reality that if a design doesn't work for the client's way of living, then it doesn't work at all."

Aesthetic judgment

Rafael and Joshua came to interior design from different creative backgrounds. Rafael spent 20 years studying Eastern-healing practices, while Joshua is an Emmy award-winning visual effects designer for film and television. "Our diverse backgrounds provide us with a unique vantage point in our collaboration," says Joshua. "We draw from an extensive set of tools and influences. It keeps life interesting."

Given FORM's experience in creating extraordinary, livable spaces, the 2015 launch of an exclusive collection of case goods, upholstery, and home accessories seems a natural evolution. "Whenever we design a home, we aim to provide our clients with something incredibly special," says Joshua. "We're expanding this vision with the launch of our first collection, which will retail across the USA, and in parts of Europe, Asia, and Australia."

Rafael adds: "We enjoy working in a variety of idioms, always mixing luxury with longevity, and style with sustainability. Put simply, we love good design and we love good form."

www.formlosangeles.com

GRAND PLANS

Harrison Design specializes in bespoke, classical architecture, which draws influence from the grand buildings of 16th-century Europe

From the age of 12, William H. Harrison spent his summers and Saturdays working in an architect's office. For him, the study and practice of architecture has been a lifelong passion.

"Architecture is never just architecture," he says. "It's part of the whole existence that we as humans thrive in."

Harrison Design, the company that William founded in 1990, is based upon classical architectural principles. Over the past 25 years, Harrison Design has created a diverse body of work—from stately homes to commercial projects—all informed by traditional techniques and proportions.

Italian inspiration

William takes particular inspiration from the works of 16th-century Venetian architect Andrea Palladio, buildings that he first experienced when travelling through Italy in his early twenties. He follows Palladio's philosophy that good design is primarily about creating spaces that are well-proportioned, flexible and adaptive.

"I walked into one of Palladio's villas," says William, "and was enamored with the space—the proportion and scale, the humanism of it. It was 500 years old and you could still live in it today. As architects we are taught to create objects, but what we should learn is how to create livable, usable space."

Another key influence is the British architect Sir Edwin Lutyens. Where Palladio inspires through the proportions of his agricultural villas and palazzi, Lutyens' work taught William the importance of context and setting. The principals at Harrison Design's practice all share a commitment to producing works of lasting value that respond to their environment.

"Good architecture is about creating a sense of place," says William. "Look at the Viceroy's House that Lutyens built in imperial Delhi. He accomplished a masterpiece by immersing himself in the local culture."

"AS ARCHITECTS WE ARE TAUGHT TO CREATE OBJECTS, BUT WHAT WE SHOULD LEARN IS HOW TO CREATE LIVABLE, USABLE SPACE"

While William and his team look to classical ideals for inspiration, their practice blends old and new concepts, and firmly embraces the technology of today. "Palladio was a master of revitalizing the classical look, but he did it in a personal way," says William. "He took the tenets of classical architecture and expressed them in his own language."

The principals and associates at Harrison Design respond to and develop their clients' visions through a full range of services. These include site planning, architectural design, interior design, landscape architecture, and construction administration and management.

A global enterprise

Over the past two decades, Harrison Design has expanded from its Atlanta base and now has offices in Santa Barbara, Los Angeles, New York, Washington D.C. and St. Simons Island. It also has an office in Shanghai, where it has partnered with local firms to bring its carefully considered design to China's booming construction industry. The opening of this first international office builds upon a number of international projects completed in Canada, Africa, the Caribbean, China, Europe, and the Middle East.

Harrison Design creates singular buildings that are purposeful, functional, and beautiful. It aims to raise the standards that other practitioners work to, and add value to individuals and communities.

"To get a well-designed home or building, you have to throw out style and ask—does it function the way it was intended to?" says William. "Will it allow itself to mature and age and still be of value? If you design that way, you can set clear parameters for what you're trying to accomplish."

www.harrisondesign.com

BLUEPRINT FOR SUCCESS

Miami-based Portuondo Perotti Architects offers an all-encompassing architectural service that remains true to its boutique origins, built upon nearly three decades of recognition

Portuondo Perotti Architects may be located in Miami, but the company has always had a global appeal. "Miami is a melting pot," says Rafael Portuondo, who cofounded the practice with Jose Perotti in 1986. "Our clients are British, Russian, South American, and a host of other nationalities, and the challenge for us is that they are all looking for something unique." As well as serving such a diverse clientele, Portuondo Perotti Architects appeals to those seeking a building that is both distinct and long-lasting.

Mostly, however, the company's appeal comes from its reputation—it is renowned for undertaking architectural projects using a detailed eye and a range of international influences. The company's portfolio of work includes many types of projects, from Tuscan-style villas to Bauhaus-influenced buildings, such as the astronomy observatory for Florida International University.

"We've done houses in the Hamptons and projects in China, but the principle is always the same," says Rafael. "Our aim is to create something beautiful, timeless, and architecturally recognizable."

Additional expertise

While the quality and detail of Portuondo Perotti Architects' buildings speak loudly for themselves, the company's attention to the site and environment in which a building lives plays a key role in each project's allure. "A lot of the houses we design and build are located on one- or two-acre lots—some have even been 100 acres," says Rafael. "We pay a lot of attention to the gardens surrounding the buildings and always incorporate them into our original drawings." With such potential living in each site, creating outstanding features in a project is a necessity for the company.

Portuondo Perotti Architects' interior design service, headed by Jordi Esteban, is equally

"THE QUALITY OF SERVICE WE OFFER AS A BOUTIQUE COMPANY IS MUCH GREATER—IT'S MORE FOCUSED, THOUGHTFUL, AND PERSONAL"

sought after. "Our mission is to make designs as magnificent inside as out," says Jordi. "It's an approach that uses detailed plans and elevation diagrams, and provides as much advice as our clients require."

Trusted and renowned

The company's expansion over the past 30 years has been dramatic. However, its founders have chosen to stay true to its boutique beginnings and the company has just 15 full-time employees. And though much has changed in the architectural community since its conception, Portuondo Perotti Architects remains committed to honoring the proven values of good design. "We've recognized that the quality of service we offer as a boutique company is much greater—it's more focused, thoughtful, and personal," says Rafael.

One thing that hasn't changed, however, is people's reaction to Portuondo Perotti Architects' designs. With return and referral work making up a significant part of the company's business, it is trusted, renowned, and recommendable. "Our clients expect projects to be completed to a certain standard," says Rafael. "They come to us because they know they'll get that level of quality, as well as something special." The company also ensures to deliver work in a timely and responsive manner, always demanding a standard of excellence from the craftsmen who execute its designs.

For Rafael, the key to continuing the company's success is to maintain an open mind and keep pushing the boundaries. "We're constantly testing each other in the office," he says. "It's what keeps our offering fresh and our ideas flowing—which is essential in satisfying the melting pot we serve."

www.portuondo-perotti.com

WISH FULFILLMENT

*Based in New York, Richard Piemonte Design Associates
creates beautiful interiors, transforming clients' ideas
from dream home to reality*

Designing the perfect home for his clients is a labor of love for Richard Piemonte of New York-based Richard Piemonte Design Associates. Whether it's an opulent traditional look or the clean lines of a contemporary style, two things remain constant: the provision of personalized service and an assurance of quality.

"I'm a firm believer in listening to my clients' needs and desires," says Richard. "Design, in my mind, is a marriage of practicality and fantasy. As a boutique operation, we recognize the importance of giving our clients' ideas and suggestions our full attention. Every project is a blank canvas on which a portrait can be painted, of who the client is, of their taste and their style."

State of the art

"Inspiration for design is everywhere," says Richard. "It could be from a painting, a piece of sculpture, a family heirloom, an antique, a photo collection, a fabulous view—or perhaps it's a favorite color that we want to incorporate. One project's colors were inspired by a collection of Mucha posters. For another, it was Frederick Remington's paintings of the Wild West."

Richard's three decades of experience ensure that every aspect of a design works in harmony. For a vacation home in Aspen, he was asked to blend the best of European and Western styles. Furniture and fittings were chosen specifically so that the two contrasting themes complimented each other. And rather than using on-trend pieces that tend to date very quickly, Richard's focus was on creating a design that evoked both comfort and timeless luxury.

With projects that range from individual rooms to major schemes that involve the entire building process, Richard and his associate,

Allyn Kandel, work with an expert team of architects, lighting specialists, and landscape designers to ensure that every aspect of the work fits the overall design plan.

"WE RECOGNIZE THE IMPORTANCE OF GIVING OUR CLIENTS' IDEAS AND SUGGESTIONS OUR FULL ATTENTION"

A detailed approach

For Richard, there is no such thing as too much attention to detail. It might involve visiting a workroom to make sure upholstery details meet specifications, or travelling to Europe with a client to choose the perfect antique or accessory—Richard is always present and hands-on. A particularly challenging project, for example, involved him spending two days with a charity to make sure that a client's home was suitable for their disabled child.

With a string of forthcoming projects that focus on contemporary décor, Richard's future work looks set to enhance his existing reputation for opulent, refined traditional interiors. But, whether it's classic or modern, the high-quality and bespoke service that he provides sets him apart.

"I consider myself fortunate when clients allow me to translate their visions into reality," says Richard. "Knowing their thoughts and feelings helps me to make their home one that suits them perfectly—and, hopefully, one that far exceeds their expectations."

A labor of love, perhaps, but one that Richard is very willing to undertake.

www.richardpiemontedesignassociates.com

HIDDEN TREASURES

Concealing complete bars inside pianos and TVs inside sideboards, Studio Becker has become the international specialist in secreted storage systems for luxury furniture

It looks—and sounds—like a grand piano. Once you get closer, however, you realize that the polished wood curves of the instrument actually house a complete bar. A true piano bar.

"We have installed an electronic keyboard, so it's a playable digital piano," says Roar Vaernes, CEO of the bespoke cabinetry company Studio Becker. "But, because it's the size of a concert grand, we have plenty of space to store stemware, liquor, a dozen wine bottles, an ice bucket, a wine cooler, bar tools—even a cigar section with an ashtray, lighter, and cigar cutters."

This unique Piano Bar serves as just one example of the kind of ingenious concealed furniture made by Studio Becker. It installs television screens that elevate from sideboards at the push of a button, or paneling that elegantly conceals storage units or office spaces. It can even fashion cosmetic refrigerators for bedrooms, or storage for valued jewelry that will emerge from behind a panel in response to a biometric fingerprint switch.

"It's a source of both pride and satisfaction for us to develop creative solutions to practical problems, as well as individual touches to suit each customer's personality," says Roar. "The more of a challenge it is, the more creative we get."

Success story

Studio Becker started out in Norway in 1946 as a family-owned firm making bathrooms. Within 30 years, it was Scandinavia's largest retail kitchen and bath business. In 1987, it set up a base in San Francisco to sell high-end European kitchens.

Soon, however, the innovative storage systems that it was building for kitchen units started to have applications around the home, and Studio Becker evolved into a manufacturer of bespoke millwork.

Functionality isn't the only essential element. "We always create a focal point," says Roar. "For instance, we like wardrobes that are concealed behind eye-catching artwork, colorful lacquer finishes, or unusual materials. We are always using new materials, materials you'd never usually dream of using in a kitchen, such as leather or fabrics. We use salmon skin for furniture in living rooms and bedrooms as it's very sustainable and versatile. We introduced carbon fiber many years ago, aluminum even earlier, and recently stingray—although we're careful to use those that are plentiful and not endangered."

Not only does Studio Becker use high-quality sustainable materials, chosen specifically for each individual project and handcrafted to perfection, but its long-standing commitment to the environment means that all products are free of formaldehyde and PVC-based plastics.

"THE MORE OF A CHALLENGE IT IS, THE MORE CREATIVE WE GET"

Luxurious living

Today, Studio Becker brings its expertise to every room of the home. It draws upon master carpenters in Germany, design specialists in Italy, and a product development team that's constantly working on new design solutions to make life "more luxurious and more organized." The resulting bespoke creations cover the entire spectrum, from traditional style to cutting-edge chic.

Now, soft furnishings are joining its existing millwork, accessories, and luggage collection, made in association with renowned Italian designers. "We initially focused on built-in pieces," says Roar. "Now we are looking at tables, chairs, and sofas to complete the home." With the company's promise of "extreme customization," customers are not limited by fixed sizes or finishes. This ensures that each item is genuinely bespoke.

And, whether these pieces are elegantly designed kitchens or ingenious piano bars, it's likely that they'll be innovative creations. For Studio Becker, the next challenge has only just begun.

www.studiobecker.com

LIFE AND STYLE

Seamlessly blending architecture, interior design, and landscaping, Studio William Hefner in Los Angeles creates homes that are as well-suited to a client's way of living as they are stunning

I can make anything beautiful—but that doesn't make it livable," says architect William Hefner. Instead, his vision lies in designing homes that fit the lifestyles of their inhabitants.

For William and his colleagues at Studio William Hefner, founded in 1989, this means spending time understanding how clients live. It involves creating connections between rooms, and between interiors and exteriors. "Clients often ask 'When are we going shopping?' but you need to get the floor plan right first," says William. "I customize homes according to a client's lifestyle, which for some people means not hearing staff clanking dishes when they're having dinner. For others, it's being in the kitchen but still being able to see the rest of the family."

Extensive research
William also carries out extensive research into the finer details of each interior. When his Los Angeles-based firm won a commission to design a 40,000-ft chateau, William and his interior-designer wife Kazuko Hoshino, a principal at Studio William Hefner, packed their suitcases and headed for France's Loire Valley along with their young son.

"You need to be like an actor rehearsing a role," says William. "If the details and preparation aren't just right, then the end result won't work. On the trip, I learned a lot about the depth and scale used in chateaux."

This dedication to research was also applied to the property's exterior, which was completed in 2014. Blending landscaping with interior design

and architectural expertise, the Studio William Hefner team created a multidimensional garden that combined grand spaces, a parterre, and a culinary garden.

Bespoke designs
Attention to detail extends also to the bespoke furniture that the firm creates. Studio William Hefner has a relationship with a select group of Los Angeles workrooms, each of which boasts its own specialities. "Custom-made furniture doesn't go out of style, unlike popular designs, which can soon become dated," says William. "And bespoke

furniture is designed specifically to fit the scale and dimensions of the room it sits in."

One of the company's signature materials is oak, which can be stained and bleached while retaining its depth, says William. The firm also mixes metals, such as bronze and brass, to add contrast and interest to furniture. From Paris-based lighting experts to stone merchants in Italy, Studio William Hefner also works with artisans in Europe to ensure that its fittings are of the finest quality. The studio's clientele is as extensive as its research is in-depth, and includes prominent businesspeople, entertainment industry executives, and customers located as far afield as the Middle East.

> "YOU NEED TO BE LIKE AN ACTOR REHEARSING A ROLE. IF THE PREPARATION ISN'T RIGHT, THEN THE END RESULT WON'T WORK"

When it came to creating their own home, William and Kazuko used the same exacting standards they apply to work projects. Details in the couple's home include steel-framed windows in the kitchen, so that no one feels cut off from guests outside, and a pair of sycamore trees in the garden to remind the couple of al fresco lunches in the South of France. "We are very satisfied customers," laughs William. Satisfied customers, with a beautiful and livable home.
www.williamhefner.com

ROOTED IN TRADITION

Duncan McRoberts Associates' classical style of architecture has earned the Pacific Northwest practice admirers in high places

Hundreds of years after they were built, the stunning Palladian masterpieces of 16th-century Venice and Regency London are as enduringly beautiful as ever. It's a tradition that award-winning architect Duncan McRoberts is continuing.

Honored as a New Palladian—one of the world's 48 leading practitioners of contemporary classical and traditional architecture—McRoberts's exquisite designs draw on the substantive principles of beauty, proportion, and craft that embody Andrea Palladio's own Venetian classics.

Today, Duncan's design firm, located in the Pacific Northwest, creates timeless and elegant architecture that befits its setting. Admirers include His Royal Highness the Prince of Wales, heir to the British throne, who shares an almost identical architectural vision and who has invited Duncan to four of his urban design task forces.

Beautiful buildings

Far from being outdated, Duncan believes the tenets of traditional design are as relevant as ever. "Beauty is integral to the ideas we aspire to as human beings," he says. "Defining beauty is complex. I would never define it in words but I always try to in built form."

Central to this is the use of the finest natural materials. "Classical architecture is about enduring craftsmanship," he says. "It transforms natural materials into high art at one with nature."

Duncan studied classical architecture in Rome and London, where he trained with world-renowned Richard H. Driehaus Prize laureate

Dr. Demetri Porphyrios. His scholarship in traditional design has also led him to become President of the Pacific Northwest chapter of the Institute of Classical Architecture & Art, and seen him become an alumnus of The Prince's Foundation.

Each bespoke structure is unique and tailored to its individual client, but his creations —be they high-end estates, country houses, or beach houses—share certain core values. "Even a small hamlet has overriding Vitruvian principles of beauty and building well," says Duncan.

The straightforwardness of his designs at Belhaven, on the Oregon coast, are a good

example. "Belhaven takes traditional design principles that I learned from The Prince's Foundation and creates architecture in harmony with nature," he says. "It is at the same time profoundly modern and timeless, and these ideals of beauty contribute to the schema of our life experiences."

Whether it's stylish simplicity or Palladian grandeur, classical foundations ensure that these designs will endure. "Traditional architecture aspires to use many variations of character, decor, and expression," says Duncan, "and will always capture the hearts of many kinds of people."
www.mcroberts-associates.com

A DESIGN FOR LIFE

With showrooms in and around Chicago, Linly Designs has been furnishing and decorating the homes of high-end clients in opulent style for the past 13 years

I've always been a big-picture person," says Janet Linly, "and the growth of the company has been hugely gratifying for me and everyone who works here." She's talking about the interior design service that she founded in 2002 in the Chicago suburbs. Since then, the company has added three showrooms and a design studio, and become a byword for classic, immaculately finished interiors with an Old World, European flavour. With the acquisition of luxury tableware and home accessories brand Tabula Tua in 2014, the company is set to expand across America.

Linly Designs features a smartly edited range of more than 250 furnishings and home accessories names, including the likes of Habersham Furniture, Marge Carson, and La Barge. The addition of Tabula Tua completes the picture. The latter's selection of the best international porcelain and tableware, such as MUD Australia, Astier de Villatte, and Reichenbach, comprises home furnishings in a contemporary French style, all of which are also available via Tabula Tua's wedding-registry service.

"We build our client relationships on results and our results always exceed expectations," says Janet. "The high-end customer wants things yesterday. Anyone can get you a painting or a rug or a floral arrangement, but to get it all fitted and perfected in 24 hours, that's what sets us apart."

Linly Designs mobilizes its team of interior designers, paint-finish experts, window treatment specialists, and carpenters in order to create entire new interior schemes in a day. "You just don't get that kind of customer 'wow' factor when a project has been worked on for months," she says.

Homes, sweet homes

The company's clients regularly commission Linly Designs to decorate their second and third homes, giving the team carte blanche to create interiors for them in keeping with their taste but with a subtly different feel for each property. "We are given the credit card and are told: 'We trust your style, just get it done as fast as possible,'" says Janet.

The next step for Linly Designs and Tabula Tua is expansion to L.A. and New York, with plans for interior design services and retail spaces. "We want to be a nationally renowned, high-end brand," says Janet. "We are known for uncompromising luxury accompanied by uncompromising design quality." Guided by the energy and excellence of her team, Janet's big picture is coming to fruition in suitably stylish fashion.

www.linlydesigns.com

CARVED CLASS

When it comes to antique European stoneware, California's Neolithic Design provides the real deal, sourcing authentic, high-quality materials for its discerning clientele

California-based company Neolithic Design specializes in supplying its US clientele with authentic European elegance for their homes. Whether remodeling a multimillion-dollar house, searching for a reclaimed limestone mantelpiece, or looking for a replica European fountain, the company has it covered.

The interior and exterior design firm sources reclaimed Mediterranean stoneworks and hand carves them to meet its clients' specific requirements. Its expert team of designers produces meticulously crafted fireplaces, grand garden fountains, intricate floorings, sinks, and colossal entryways—all from the highest quality limestone. These works of art are on display in Neolithic Design's showrooms in Los Angeles and Newport Beach, as well as on its website.

The company is also adept at tackling bespoke projects. One couple, for instance, fell in love with a 17th-century fountain that they came across while on vacation in France. Once home, they commissioned Neolithic Design to make a smaller, but proportionately accurate, version for their garden. And when an Italian client wanted his family coat of arms added to his custom-carved limestone mantel, Neolithic Design did just that, armed with only his surname. The end result added a personal touch—as well as a piece of history—to his home.

Mediterranean originals
"We reclaim a lot of our architectural elements from the Mediterranean," says owner Erwin Gutenkunst. "Many of our clients have lived in Europe or traveled extensively around it. They come to us because they want to have that authentic European feel both inside and outside their homes.

"The design is very important, but so is selecting the right stone," he adds. "We deal with the densest limestone on the market. By carving our products out of the highest quality stone, we know they will withstand extreme temperatures and last for centuries.

"We're known for our customer service as well as our excellent products," he continues. "Most people we encounter are working on their first house, so we give them all the guidance they need." Erwin and his team are also skilled at blending decorative styles, so they can combine the old with the new seamlessly.

And no project is too big or too small. Whether customers go to Neolithic Design to remodel their high-end home or to source a small feature stone, they know they'll come away with a piece of history and a work of art that will be appreciated for generations to come.
www.neolithicdesign.com

A PLACE IN THE SUN

Versatile architectural firm Timothy James Slawson
designs dream residences to a client's specific tastes
in the enticing Florida Keys

Sun-soaked and tropical, the Florida Keys is a haven for those in search of a first home, or even a second home. People from around the world are drawn to its climate and natural beauty.

Indeed, many clients of the Florida Key's architect Timothy James Slawson are seeking refuge from colder climates in Europe and across America, Canada, and beyond.

Tim set up his firm in 2001, initially working from his dining table, and now has three employees. He is a member of the American Institute of Architects and has established a loyal, word-of-

mouth following. Working in partnership with clients and interior designers, the practice creates around four to eight luxury homes per year in the Keys. Both new and remodeled structures, the residences range from 4,500 to 6,500 sq ft and are all air-conditioned.

"Our mission is to create a style based upon the clients' wishes rather than what we deem to be stylish," says Tim. "It's the client's home, not ours." This means that there are no limits to the design possibilities available, and has led to a diverse portfolio. Tim's team has designed

homes in a huge variety of styles, including Moroccan, Old Florida, Bermuda, West Indies, Caribbean, and classic Key West styles.

Standout properties

One of the most impressive was a 12,500 sq ft Balinese-style home, completed in 2007 in Key Largo, which featured in *Open House* magazine in 2008. "My clients wanted a tropical and highly landscaped five-bedroom house that opened up like a pod," says Tim. "They wanted to feel like they were living in Bali."

This Balinese pod design incorporated open-plan spaces with high ceilings, pools, water features, large overhangs, and mature landscaping. The pool was integrated into the center of the house, and it was possible to see from the living room through to the bedroom. In addition, the stunning entrance had custom hand-carved wood doors, and used local stone and cypress. The house had no rain gutters; instead, sheets of rain enveloped the house and provided a natural cooling system.

Tim's designs are consistently clean and simple with good proportions and eco-friendly principles, such as cross ventilation for natural cooling and to minimize use of air conditioning. Local materials are also used, such as coral rock —a keystone material—and cypress.

The company's expertise and versatile use of local materials ensure that wherever in the world clients find inspiration, the end result is always a place to call home.
www.timothyjamesslawsonarchitecture.com

Chapter 4
OBJECTS OF DESIRE

STROKES OF GENIUS

With his New York Concierge Gallery Ackerman's Fine Art,
Kenny Ackerman is spreading his love and enthusiasm for fine
art to a diverse and discriminating clientele

In the elegant suburb of Purchase, half an hour's drive from New York City, is a hidden gem for discerning collectors of fine art. Ackerman's Fine Art is owned and run by its founder Kenny Ackerman, whose love of paintings lured him away from a 20-year career on Wall Street to specialize in buying and selling significant artworks as a collector and private dealer.

Kenny personally buys all the paintings that he sells, making his knowledge and diligence vital to the success of the business. "I do not purchase any piece with questionable authenticity because I am personally taking the risk," he says. "And, because I share a passion for art with my clients, I only buy what I like."

Aside from the pleasure that paintings bring, there are sound economic reasons for buying from Ackerman's. "Art, as an investment, is doing very well," says Kenny. "It is a by-product of the present economic situation and the improving stock market. Art holds intrinsic value, like real estate."

An industry innovator
Ackerman's—a Concierge Gallery & Private Collection Advisor—has no storefront, and much of its business is conducted by appointment or through its attractive and detailed website. Having a substantially less expensive operating model, Kenny is able to pass savings to his clients, adding value to their purchases.

"If you walk into a New York City gallery and see a painting offered at $300,000," says Kenny, "you would very likely be able to make the purchase from me at 20 to 40 percent less, simply because I operate more efficiently. Private transactions, without buyers' and sellers' premiums, more accurately reflect the painting's actual worth."

Ackerman's also provides safety and reliability to sellers with legal documentation, guaranteed prompt payment, and bonded shipping at no extra charge. For buyers, Ackerman's offers a guaranteed investment policy that enables customers to refresh their collections with an exchange credit of the original purchase price. In addition, he offers to add a minimum of three percent of the original price per year of ownership to the gallery's valued, repeat clients.

The real thing
Authenticity has always been a concern for collectors of fine art. Ackerman's addresses this squarely by guaranteeing the validity of the works sold, with a pledge to give an immediate refund should any turn out not to be genuine. "That has never happened," says Kenny, "but it adds peace of mind for the collector."

> "BECAUSE I SHARE A PASSION
> FOR ART WITH MY CLIENTS,
> I ONLY BUY WHAT I LIKE"

Kenny has developed his personal collection with many pieces that are in common with the interests of his clientele, and he has a novel way of testing the potential of an artwork. "Occasionally, I bring a painting to my home to experience it as my clients would," he says. "It allows me the ability to better know the power of a specific work."

It is clear from a long list of testimonials that his customers enjoy the experience of dealing with Ackerman's, and many return time and again.

"It is simple, really," he says. "I respect this business as a lover of fine art myself. I wake up excited every day to find a special work that will become something wonderful for one of my valued clients."

www.ackermansfineart.com

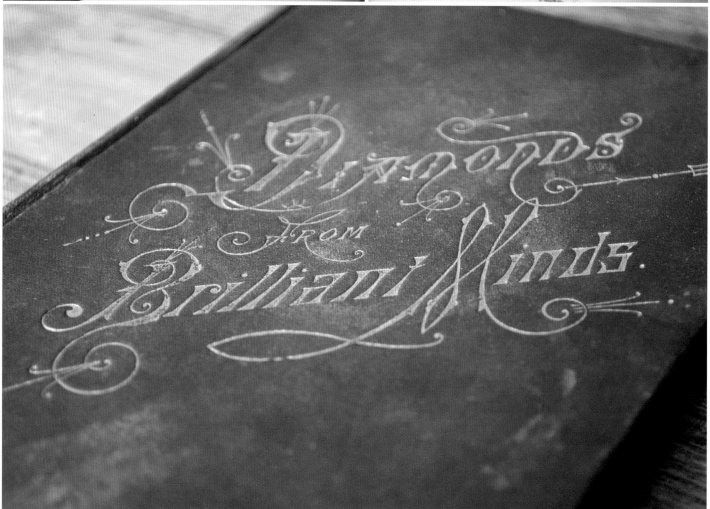

PAPERS OF NOTE

For more than 130 years, New York stationer
Dempsey & Carroll has been connecting people
through bespoke, personalized papers

While the 21st century has revealed an unbreakable bond between human beings and technology, it has also become clear that people crave genuine personal connection more deeply than ever before.

"The handwritten note fits elegantly into the anatomy of correspondence," says Jennifer Pool, President of the historic stationer Dempsey & Carroll. "It lends a sincere, emotional, and authentic connection to the recipient."

It was in 1878 that engraver John Dempsey and businessman George Carroll—describing themselves as "Art Stationers, Engravers and Publishers of Works on Social Etiquette"—set out to establish an unrivaled bespoke experience in correspondence, social, and entertaining papers. In the process, an American tradition of fine engraving and social etiquette was born.

An American institution

The first showroom and factory was located in Union Square on Manhattan's 14th Street. Nearly 14 decades later, Dempsey & Carroll—still headquartered in New York City—is hand-engraving bespoke papers for a global clientele on 100 percent cotton fiber rag milled in the USA.

"It's all about the refined texture of the paper, the hand-painted edges, the custom designed envelope finishes, the deep bruise that comes from authentic embossing," says Jennifer. "The detailed nuances of each bespoke piece—and the words that alight the pages—cannot be duplicated via any known technology. A voice echoes from the pages of a note while the recipient begins to smile. Every note—whether written with sympathy, longing, or joy—invokes a deep, emotional response."

Dempsey & Carroll is proud of its hand-made tradition. The process often begins with the commissioning of a one-of-a-kind vignette,

first drawn in pen and ink and then transferred by hand to a copper plate or steel die.

"The finishing of the product makes each piece within one suite truly unique," says Jennifer. "Each embossing of the hand-engraved plate is slightly different than the next. This variance is part of the design aesthetic. Any one of our pieces may have been made in the late 1800s."

"WE'RE WORKING IN AN AGE WHERE THE HANDWRITTEN NOTE IS, ONCE AGAIN, BECOMING THE CORNERSTONE"

The commissioning process has been passed on from generation to generation. Personal correspondence, wedding invitations, births, and sympathy announcements from Dempsey & Carroll comprise just some of the embossed papers that adorn the houses of the personalities that mark American history, and those who embrace the art of the handwritten note.

Marking moments

"The creation of each product is a journey for the client," says Jennifer. "They come to discover what it is about themselves or their loved ones that they want to celebrate. Each detail is a reflection of who they are and perhaps a bit more of who they want to be."

The most extraordinary experience is the creation of a birth announcement—where the expectant family must create a mark for a person they have yet to meet. It is a joyful and emotional process, one that involves selecting the appropriate ribbon, the right color paper, the ink, the typestyle, and—most importantly—the motif that will forever be associated with their little bundle of joy.

"We're working in an age where the handwritten note is, once again, becoming the cornerstone," says Jennifer. "We are riding the tide. The digital shift makes communication more prevalent. The receipt of a hand-finished letter makes it more special and more enduring."
www.dempseyandcarroll.com

MASSAGE MASTER

Since 1962, Inada has been making luxury chairs that mechanically replicate the effects of a shiatsu massage and provide complete comfort for all body types

It's no coincidence that so many people are evangelical about the benefits of shiatsu massage. "It's a 15-minute vacation every day; an escape," says Cliff Levin, President of Inada USA. And as Cliff knows, an Inada Massage Chair can provide a shiatsu massage any time of day or night. "Your chair will take you anywhere you want to go, chill you out, and make you calm."

A Japanese form of physiotherapy, shiatsu and its techniques are thousands of years old. Nichimu Inada, the Osaka-based businessman who founded the company in 1962, has replicated those ancient techniques with the help of an expert team of engineers and the guidance of Dr. Hideyo Matsuura, a shiatsu massage master with decades of experience.

"When you buy an Inada Massage Chair, you get Dr. Matsuura's massage expertise," says Cliff. "We can't claim the chair is a stand-in for a human, but you can expect an experience that takes the therapeutic possibilities of a home massage chair to a new level."

Back to nature

Being hunched over in front of a computer all day is a hazard of modern-day working, with the potential to cause back problems.

However, Inada's latest designs, including the enhanced version of its signature DreamWave and the posture-focused Flex 3s, incorporate proprietary scanning technology that locates an individual's pressure points, compares the results with 106 stored body profiles, and then gives a customized shiatsu massage based on the body type. Each chair adjusts to fit different heights, with the overall aim being to create a fully bespoke massage.

"Mr. Inada is committed to creating groundbreaking advances in technology and capability, and to craftsmanship," says Cliff.

"The quest for perfection is such that many prototypes are rejected by the technical team."

Such is the popularity of Inada Massage Chairs that international sales have grown to 150,000 a year. Indeed, 2014 saw the Colorado-based company make *Inc* magazine's list of the top 5,000 fastest-growing private companies in the US. The vast majority of sales are to those wanting the chairs for home use, although clients also include chiropractic clinics and spas.

Health and relaxation

According to Cliff, people either buy a massage chair purely for relaxation or to help treat a health issue such as back pain or insomnia. "We have pure luxury buyers—with disposable income—that want a massage chair and want the best. We also have people with health needs."

There are numerous research studies that demonstrate the medical benefits of massage therapy. In fact, Inada carried out its own research on massage chairs available in Japan, and concluded that regular sessions can result in a decline in heart rate as well as a reduction in levels of stress hormones in the bloodstream. "We truly believe the massage chair experience can deliver a number of therapeutic benefits," says Cliff.

> "WE TRULY BELIEVE THE MASSAGE CHAIR EXPERIENCE CAN DELIVER A NUMBER OF THERAPEUTIC BENEFITS"

Durability, reliability, and elegance are all qualities that Inada strives to achieve in its chairs. Where some companies may be quick to bring out new models, Inada likes to "future-proof" its products. Indeed, the company is committed to developing chairs that last 24 years or more. "We're always looking at new technology but investment is slow and deliberate," says Cliff. "When you buy quality, it's going to serve you for a long time."

For Inada customers, that means many hours enjoying a relaxing massage experience. Dr. Matsuura can be truly proud.
www.inadausa.com

A SOUND INVESTMENT

Each of McPherson Guitars' acoustic masterpieces is a creation
of note, whether commissioned to reflect an individual's passion
for playing or as a unique work of instrumental art

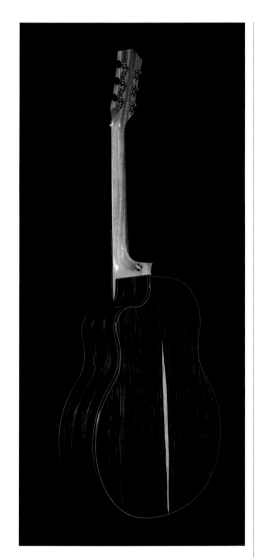

A Picasso painting, a nautical scene, and two marble turtles are just three of the motifs that have been brought to life on McPherson Guitars' bespoke creations.

However, the features that make this company unique are far from purely decorative. Born to a musical family, founder Matt McPherson grew up experimenting with guitar shapes and qualities,

"WE DON'T PAINT OR STAIN ANYTHING. IF WE WANT RED, WE USE QUEBRACHO WOOD FROM ARGENTINA, OR BLOOD WOOD"

dedicating years to improving upon the traditional guitar model. "Music is one of the loves of his life," says General Manager Larry Klenc, "and he has developed a near-perfect guitar."

The Wisconsin-based firm carefully crafts just 150 of these instruments a year. Key features include the off-center sound hole, cantilevered neck, and carbon re-enforcement. Customers can also customize a one-of-a-kind piece, which can cost anything up to $100,000. "We let people make their guitar their own," says Larry.

For starters, clients from all over the world can select the exact example of exotic wood they want their guitar to be made from. The next step is the inlay: "We don't paint or stain anything," says Larry. "If we want red, for example, we use quebracho wood from Argentina, or blood wood, which is a burgundy color." As for the imagery, "a customer might have a theme in mind," he explains, "or they might work with our artists on a design that is right for them."

The art of the axe
Understandably, most buyers want to play their finished instrument. "But some people just want to own one," Larry smiles. "We recently made a guitar that was a reproduction of a 1912 Picasso painting using 425 hand-cut, hand-placed pieces. It took 12 months to complete—and the lady that bought it doesn't even play! She owns a Picasso, so we built a display case with Picasso-esque curves and angles, and everything tilted sideways. The guitar was bought as a piece of art." A week later, her husband commissioned one with a ship motif. He doesn't play either.

McPherson is a company driven by such projects and personalities. "We build lasting relationships with our customers," says Larry.

"Take the inlay artist, for example, who works one-to-one with each client, carefully crafting artwork and emailing design ideas back and forth. We take our time in order to get it right."

Should a client require a face-to-face meeting, McPherson is happy to go the extra mile. "We've flown people to our workshop at our expense, picked them up at the airport, and put them up in the best hotel," says Larry. "That's how we do things. Sometimes we'll send them a box of chocolate-dipped strawberries just to say thanks for being our customer. Little things like that mean we can work together to create masterpieces."

Customer satisfaction
As for the future, as well as the McPherson six-string, 12-string, and smaller Camrielle model, the company is working on a parlor guitar. There's also the Kevin Michael Travel Guitar, a carbon-fiber instrument that's lightweight, heatproof, and waterproof. "You can take it on a picnic, hunting, camping, or fishing," says Larry. "You can leave it in the back of your car. And we will be doing customization too, with paint jobs and digital printing." This colorful collection will launch later this year.

So, what about the turtles? "A customer came to us requesting something from a 1970 Grateful Dead album," says Larry. "We wanted to create something elegant, so we researched the record and found a motif of two turtles. They were dancing and one was playing a banjo while the other was playing a tambourine, so we recreated that image using green marble.

"Nobody else in the world has a guitar like that," says Larry. "Now, when he shows it to his friends, they know it's absolutely unique."
www.mcphersonguitars.com

FLAWLESS PROPORTIONS

Designed with an ideal balance between form and function,
Ratio's coffee makers produce the perfect blend to help combat
the daily grind

Coffee makers are not usually built to last. "Most of them are more or less disposable," says Mark Hellweg, founder of the Oregon-based company Ratio. "Our machines, however, were created out of an opportunity to create something iconic. We're inspired by the expertise and thought behind design classics, such as the Eames lounger and Rolls-Royce cars, and we focus on balancing three key concepts: beauty, quality, and coffee."

The result is an elegant machine called Eight, whose simple design automates the complexity of producing pour-over coffee. Its three-step process allows grounds to bloom, extracting subtle flavors in the coffee, while sensors automatically detect the brewing time needed and maintain the water at the ideal temperature of 202°F.

A design classic

"To make a similar cup of coffee manually, you'd need to distribute water regularly in a circular motion so it doesn't get too high or low—this would require a scale, a pouring kettle, and a timer," says Mark. "We're inspired by the way the motion enhances the coffee, but have the Eight take care of temperature and bloom cycle. Our software optimizes the time and contact between water and coffee, in a beautiful, iconic design. When the machine makes it, it's as simple as pressing one button."

Eight's elegant build was developed using only high-quality components. Black walnut accents are sourced in Oregon, while precision die-cast aluminum parts, machined to one-tenth of a millimeter, are manufactured in a factory that also produces fighter jet components.

Ratio's most impressive design feat was creating four unique lab-grade blown borosilicate glass parts for each machine. Eight's glass features require artisan glass specialists in both the Czech Republic and China to ensure a perfect fit and finish. "The tolerances are very tight and it has to be exactly the right size," says Mark. "There's a reason most coffee makers are plastic; a design like ours is very difficult and very expensive to create. By committing ourselves to the use of natural materials, we set ourselves up for a big challenge —but it is one that we were willing to face."

"RATIO FOCUSES ON BALANCING THREE KEY CONCEPTS: BEAUTY, QUALITY, AND COFFEE"

Considered detailing

Even the smallest details of Eight have been considered, from an ergonomic heat stopper to a rare earth magnet housed in the base of the machine.

"We spent a lot of time thinking what it would be like to use, so as to create an incredibly intuitive design," says Mark. "We have customers in their 20s who are very tech-savvy but—at the same time—I'm designing a machine for my 83-year-old grandmother to simply open up, add coffee and water, and brew."

With more than a thousand orders placed before final production began, Ratio's focus is firmly on its stylish Eight coffee machine for the time being. But Mark already plans to develop the line in the future: "All products will have a similar distinctive design language, but we'll look at different colors, as well as other materials such as stone, leather, and different woods, as well as limited-edition versions—possibly even grinders. We know that there will be other opportunities, and that the potential for this fantastic product is almost limitless."

With its blend of top-quality materials, strikingly good looks, and unbeatable coffee, the brand's journey to iconic status is well underway.

www.ratiocoffee.com

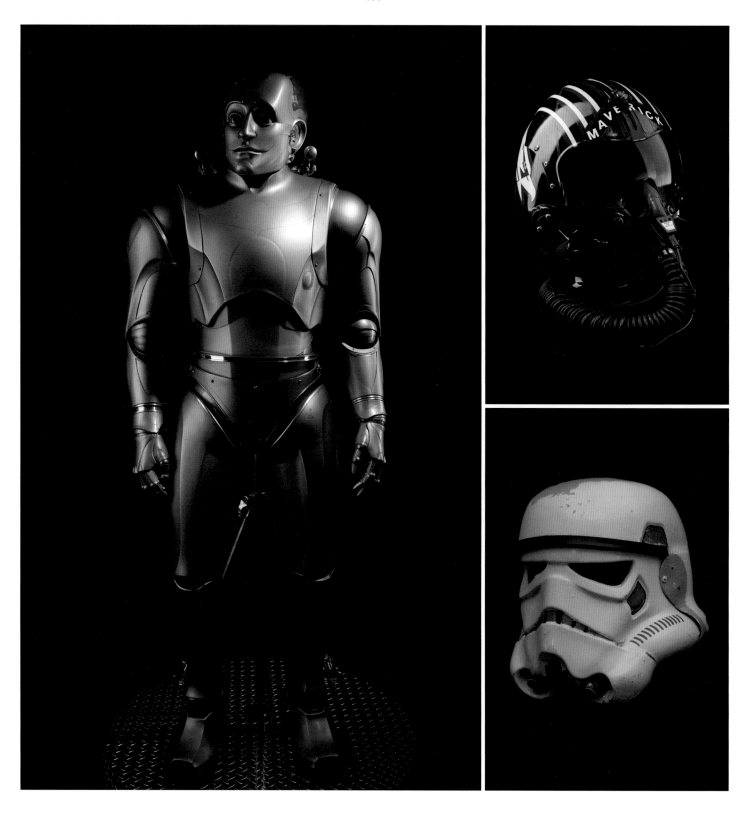

HOLLYWOOD HISTORY

Whether it's a Star Trek script, Darth Vader's helmet, or Keanu Reeves's suit from Constantine, ScreenUsed can help its customers find their very own slice of movie memorabilia

Turning a passion into a business takes courage. To be successful, though, an entrepreneur needs to establish the right contacts—and Desi DosSantos has spent years doing just that.

With his partner Jeff Castillo, Desi runs ScreenUsed, an internet-based retailer that sells props, costumes, and special effects that have been used during Hollywood movie and television production. Walter White's yellow jumpsuit complete with gas mask from the hit series *Breaking Bad* and Freddy Krueger's legendary razor glove from *Nightmare on Elm Street* are among the items that the California-based pair have acquired for enthusiasts. They source their memorabilia from an international network of contacts including costumers, wardrobe houses, and prop professionals. "It's not like stamp-collecting," says Desi. "You can't just go into a shop or walk onto a set. You need to know the right people."

Movie memorabilia

Jeff and Desi founded the firm in 2003 in San Jose, but the concept behind ScreenUsed was developed in the 1990s. Already an avid collector, Desi was looking for a hoverboard from *Back to the Future*. He found one on eBay but couldn't believe it was real, so he called the supplier and went on to buy it. "Like a lot of people, I didn't know you could own a piece of a movie," he says. "That's when I started getting in touch with prop guys myself for my collection."

As well as having the right contacts, ScreenUsed has a firmly established reputation for authenticity with its worldwide client base. That means turning down up to 70 percent of items offered because Desi can't prove they're genuine. All items also come with a Certificate Of Authenticity and a money-back guarantee. "I don't want to put my name to it unless I know it's absolutely real," says Desi, who also researches items on sites including the online database IMDb. "Reputation is our entire business—if I don't have a reputation then I can't sell anything."

"LIKE A LOT OF PEOPLE, I DIDN'T KNOW YOU COULD OWN A PIECE OF A MOVIE"

The pair's clients include people wanting a piece of memorabilia to "dress" their home cinemas. Others are after specific items, which Desi and Jeff will take years looking for, such as a Darth Vader helmet. Rather than looking for "buyers," Desi and Jeff match a collector with a specific item that they'll treasure.

Caretakers of the lost art

"We're looking for 'caretakers,' which means providing the personal touch from sourcing the item to packing and shipping it ourselves," says Desi. "It's like having an art gallery and, when you get a piece you know a customer will like, you call them."

Harrison Ford's hat from *Raiders of the Lost Ark* is one of the most expensive items ScreenUsed has sold. It had belonged to Desi who had insisted he would never sell it—until he had a call from a collector offering a substantial sum. "I knew I had to move on and find a new caretaker," says Desi. "At least I know where the hat is and that it's being taken care of."

ScreenUsed is one of the most established businesses of its kind. But Desi and Jeff have no plans to expand. "We stay small," says Desi. "We aren't just warehousing stuff or throwing jackets on eBay. It's a passion first and a business second." For Desi, taking the time to invest in what he loves has certainly paid off.

www.screenused.com

ART MEETS SCIENCE

Telescopes of Vermont produces stunning sculptural telescopes and sundials, reviving a design rarity of the 1920s to create a conversation piece that brings wonder to any outdoor setting

If sitting outside on a balmy summer evening staring up at the stars seems as close to magic as real life can get, try adding a telescope. Then try adding the Porter Garden Telescope.

Originally designed in the 1920s by Russell W. Porter—the American "father of amateur astronomy"—this intricate art nouveau design is both beautiful and multifunctional; it is a telescope, a sundial, and a sculpture. It's also pretty rare. Around 55 were made in its initial incarnation—one of which is in the Smithsonian. Years later, engineer and amateur astronomer Fred Schleipman of Vermont happened upon one.

"My father thought it was gorgeous, and he had ideas on how to improve on it," says Russ Schleipman, Telescopes of Vermont's President. However, replacing the lost patterns proved to be a devilishly tricky undertaking, while the resultant castings were fraught with gremlins. "Bronze castings are like cherry pies; they look the same but they vary, especially when you're concerned with tenths of thousands of an inch. They shrink and warp as they cool."

A design reborn

Eventually, Fred convinced the Hartness-Porter Astronomy Museum in Vermont to give him a shot at it, and they lent him their Porter Telescope for just three weeks in 2006. With pattern maker Ted Nugent he gleaned the salient data, digitized it, and spent a year designing patterns and fixtures. Bert Willard and James Daley, two military satellite optics designers in Massachusetts, brought their wizardry to bear on modern mirrors and eyepieces.

And so Telescopes of Vermont was born, producing an edition of 200 bespoke, serial-numbered Garden Telescopes. "They seduce people," says Russ. "They're beautiful. You could have a Henry Moore in your garden and people would certainly acknowledge it, but the telescope will trigger a much longer conversation and become an entertainment, a favorite destination. Your guests will initially perceive it as a sculpture. Then you show them the sundial, and they're fascinated. Then you take out the custom-made leather briefcase, put in the optics and show them Jupiter, and they're blown away! There's always the same reaction: three or four seconds of silence and then a whispered 'oh my god.' It happens every time." Hardly surprising, then, that Telescopes of Vermont has some high-profile customers from the worlds of entertainment, finance, business, and government. All of them have been seduced by the bronze lady, or Capella, as the telescope was dubbed by the celebrated astronomer Sir Patrick Moore.

New products

Telescopes of Vermont's vision is key to its success, and it has not only revived the Porter Telescope, but also improved it and developed a second product—a birdbath sundial. "The products echo each other," says Russ. "The pedestal is almost identical, and the dish and the sundial 'gnomon' —the bit that casts the shadow—are based on the elements of the telescope." A third product is on the horizon, too. "Porter drew another telescope, similar to the Garden Telescope, but the long blade is replaced by a tapered tube that holds a glass lens, which converts the reflecting telescope into a refracting telescope. It's like a car that turns into an airplane. It's the ultimate gadget."

> "YOUR GUESTS SEE THAT IT IS A SCULPTURE. THEN YOU SHOW THEM THE SUNDIAL AND THEY'RE FASCINATED"

Combining innovation with a deep-rooted respect for Porter's work, the Schleipmans create their science-meets-art pieces with absolute joy. "When we show our products, I know it's an experience that people will remember," says Russ. "Older generations are amazed, kids are excited. It's best when the fireflies are out on a warm evening. We show people the moon as they've never seen it before. It is a simple, delightful experience, a magic show."
www.gardentelescopes.com

Chapter 5
CONNOISSEUR

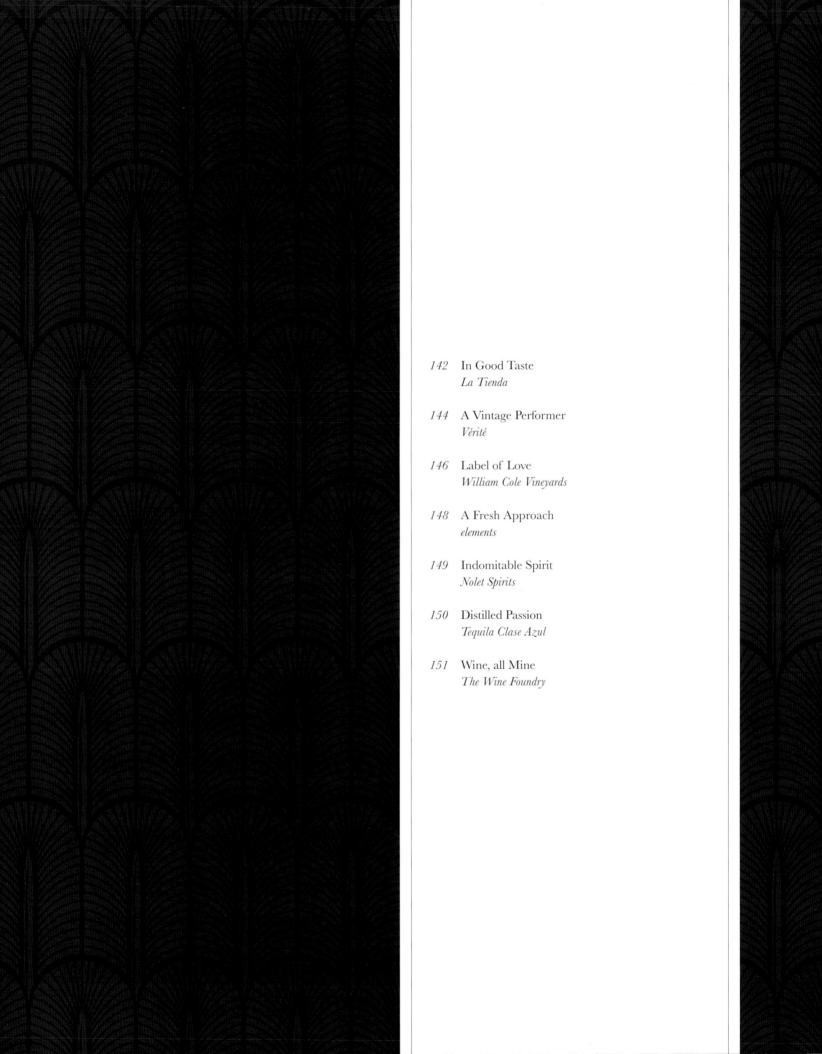

IN GOOD TASTE

With a passionate family at its helm, Virginia-based La Tienda offers the best and largest selection of artisan Spanish foods online

Over the last decade or so, the traditional flavors and ingredients of authentic Spanish cuisine have begun to take their rightful place in the US culinary firmament. One of the cuisine's key exponents is the Harris family of Williamsburg, Virginia, whose business La Tienda has supplied the USA and Canada with the finest Spanish foods since 1996.

"A distinguishing characteristic of Spanish cuisine is that it's very wholesome," says Tim Harris, La Tienda's CEO. "The emphasis, first and foremost, is on the quality of the raw ingredients. Every region has its own specialties and the people are extremely proud of what they produce."

Pioneering importers
The Harris family's love of Spanish food and culture began while living in Andalucía in the 1970s, and the family continues to think of Spain as a second home. La Tienda was the first company to sell Jamón Serrano (Spanish cured ham) in the USA, made by the curing house Redondo Iglesias. It then worked tirelessly for around eight years with ham masters at Fermìn to attain USDA approval to import the exceptional Jamón Ibérico.

Regarded by many as the very best of Europe's varied traditional hams, Jamón Ibérico comes from a breed of pig known as *pata negra*—meaning "black hoof"—which is descended from the wild black pigs that roamed the Iberian Peninsula before human settlement. Cured for between 24 and 48 months, the jamón loses around half of its weight in the process, resulting in a deep red color, distinctive marbling, and a complex taste. "The very best of this style of ham is known as Jamón Ibérico de Bellota and comes from pigs that are free to roam the forests of the dehesa," says Tim. "They gorge themselves on acorns from oak and cork trees. It is sustainable agriculture at its most basic." An exclusive, artisanal product, Jamón Ibérico de Bellota retails at around $1,000 for a whole ham.

"The importance of jamón in Spanish cuisine cannot be overstated," explains Tim. "When people entertain with a whole jamón, it becomes the focal point of the party. It allows each person to share the spirit of generosity and the food traditions that define Spain." In keeping with La Tienda's commitment to premium quality, skilled professional ham slicers—known as *cortadores*—are flown in from Spain by Cinco Jotas, Spain's elite jamón brand, throughout the year.

> "SPANISH CUISINE IS VERY WHOLESOME. THE EMPHASIS IS ON THE QUALITY OF THE RAW INGREDIENTS"

Artisanal producers
However, La Tienda is about much more than just jamón. The company imports around 1,000 products selected from more than 80 artisans, including cheeses, chorizos, olives, saffron, paella essentials, olive oils, and even par-baked bread from Galicia. Many of the small family businesses it works with had never exported before being approached by La Tienda, and the company supports them from its offices in Valencia and San Sebastián. Tim's brother, Jonathan, president and creative director at La Tienda, regularly travels the back roads of Spain to personally select each new product that La Tienda carries.

"For our Spanish customers who now live in the USA, there are few things as evocative as the foods of their childhood and their home country," says Tim. "So when we're able to bring in foods that they've not had for 10, 20, even 30 years—well, their reactions are very satisfying."
www.latienda.com

A VINTAGE PERFORMER

Sonoma County winery Vérité has proved that California
can make red wines that are every bit as good—or even
better—than their Bordeaux counterparts

Sonoma County, in California, is one of the most established wine-producing regions in the world. Its vineyards are hand-tended, hand-pruned, and hand-harvested. More than 50 grape varieties thrive here and it was named one of *Wine Enthusiast*'s 10 Best Wine Travel Destinations for 2014.

Thanks to the region's unique environment, some of Sonoma's wines, such as those produced by Vérité in Healdsburg, are compared to the best of Bordeaux. Vérité, meaning truth, has more than wine in common with the famous French region, though. Frenchman Pierre Seillan— who spent two decades as technical director and winemaker for seven Bordeaux chateaux— is the company's *vigneron*. And today, using the region's exceptional *terroir*, small vineyards, and excellent grapes, Pierre crafts three outstanding Bordeaux-style blends for the label: La Muse (Merlot-based), La Joie (Cabernet Sauvignon-based), and Le Désir (Cabernet Franc-based). Each of these is inspired by corresponding Bordeaux red-wine regions: Pomerol, Pauillac, and Saint-Émilion, respectively.

Reign of terroir

"When Jess Jackson invited me to work with him to create world-class wine in 1997, he said he wanted to make a Merlot as good as the top Bordeaux," says Pierre, of Vérité's founder. "I took one look at Sonoma County soils and said: 'Why not better?' Every hillside, every elevation and aspect offers us a different micro-cru—a vineyard within a vineyard—and the pure expression of these unique sites has defined our winemaking philosophy from the beginning."

The county's topography is extremely complex, with more diversity in the soil than elsewhere in California. Stretching from the Pacific Ocean to the Mayacamas Mountains that separate Napa from Sonoma County with valleys in between, much of the land has rocky soils created by ancient volcanic activity that stress the vines, resulting in smaller berries with more intense flavors. "We work with a palette of more than 40 soil types," says Pierre, "which results in distinct micro-crus."

The unique climate also plays its part in the wines' success due to the proximity of Sonoma County to the Pacific Ocean, whose breeze cools the soil at night, enabling the vines to recover from the heat of the day. This—along with the maritime fog from the coast that blankets many vineyards —preserves the acidity and complexity of the fruit.

> "OUR FOUNDER WANTED TO MAKE A MERLOT AS GOOD AS THE TOP BORDEAUX. I SAID: 'WHY NOT BETTER?'"

Grape expectations

The fruit for Vérité comes from its premier mountain vineyards and Pierre is involved from the first budding of the fruit to crushing so that he can understand intimately its potential to contribute to the three wines. Lots are first vinified by micro-cru, then transferred to barrels to settle and begin maceration. As the wine evolves for 15 to 18 months in new French oak barrels, Pierre tastes each lot over a period of months and decides its ultimate destination: whether La Muse, La Joie, or Le Désir.

It's an approach that works. Wine critic Robert Parker Jr. of *The Wine Advocate* awarded a total of seven perfect 100-point scores to Vérité in 2007, and since then the publication has given all three blends consistently high scores each year.

Part of Vérité's success is that—because of the barreling process—its wines have depth without having excessively strong flavors. "The oak should be like a ghost," says Pierre, "you sense its presence, but you don't actually perceive it." Blending Pierre Seillan's expertise and Sonoma's exceptional terroir, Vérité is certainly making its presence felt on the world stage.

www.veritewines.com

LABEL OF LOVE

Born and raised in the Napa Valley to a family of wine experts,
William Ballentine of William Cole Vineyards was destined
to make great wines laden with heart and history

Top-of-the-range Cabernet flows through William Ballentine's veins. The fourth generation in a family of winemakers, his father's side of the family has owned vineyards in California's Napa Valley since 1922 and his maternal great-grandfather started a winery in the valley around 1906.

"I grew up surrounded by the production of, and love of, wine, and always knew that this is what I wanted to do," says William, owner of William Cole Vineyards. Like his family before him, William's winery is also located in Napa Valley—a place whose rich history is dominated by winemaking, and whose reputation as a winegrowing region is world-class.

A life in wine

Having grown up on the family vineyard, William studied business and finance, with enology and viticulture at college. After graduation, he built up experience at a number of prominent local vineyards, honing his harvesting and blending techniques. And when what is now the William Cole Estate—a 19th-century ghost winery in St. Helena—came up for sale in 1999, he snapped it up. "I used to play here as a child," he says. "I want it to be the icon property for the Napa Valley."

However, the winery had been closed since prohibition and re-opening its doors meant hard work. Keen to maintain the original integrity of the building, William and his wife, Jane, began an extensive renovation of the stone wine cellar, while moving into its top two floors with their children, Cole and Claire.

By 2004, with the renovation complete, the couple launched their first wine: the Cuvée Claire, named after their daughter. At $175 a bottle, William personally ensures the highest standards. "I'm the only one who touches the wine," he says. "We barrel-age for over 30 months in 100 percent French oak. Then I blend the different lots until it's absolutely perfect. We bottle and pack by hand.

It's a slow and gentle process. The priority is on the taste and on maximizing quality."

In addition to the Cuvée Claire, the winery expanded its range in 2010 with a small production of Chardonnay, Cuvée Jane Marie—named after his wife. There's also TEN, an exquisite blend of 10 Cabernet Sauvignon vintages. Each product is available only from the winery, meaning its audience is select, loyal, and, in return, treated exceptionally.

> ## "I GREW UP SURROUNDED BY WINEMAKING. I ALWAYS KNEW THIS IS WHAT I WANTED TO DO"

A rich history

As well as producing superb wines, the beautiful William Cole Estate has been nominated for a place on the National Register of Historic Places. "People come for the wine and stay to see the place," says William. "There is so much history and it's crucial for us to continue telling its incredible story."

It's a story that starts in 1869, when businessman John Weinberger bought the original 240-acre estate and built a vineyard. In 1882, however, John's death at the hands of an ex-employee meant that his widow, Hannah, took over operations—becoming the first female winemaker and owner in American history.

"She kept the winery going for 38 years until prohibition," says William. "She passed away in the mid-1930s and her son sold the estate. The house's grounds are just as historic and were designed by renowned landscape architect Thomas Church, the "godfather of landscape gardening."

The winery is now open by appointment, and William's goal has always been "to preserve its history and character." The product comes first, though. "Making premium-quality wine in the area I love," he says. "I was born to do it."

www.williamcolevineyards.com

A FRESH APPROACH

*Scott Anderson's two New Jersey restaurants—elements
and Mistral—provide diners with fine dining and an
informal interpretation of his exceptional seasonal cuisine*

Scott Anderson's view of cooking as an art form has given birth to a brand-new concept: interpretive American cuisine. Inspired by a childhood spent in Japan, Scott loves exploring different texture combinations to create unusual flavors at his two restaurants in Princeton, New Jersey.

A two-time James Beard Award semifinalist, Scott constantly adapts his menus to the changing seasons. His creative approach to cuisine also ensures that any of the dishes that he serves can be adapted easily according to a customer's dietary requirements. As a result of this tailored attitude toward ingredients and personal preferences, foodie website Opinionated about Dining regularly ranks Scott's restaurant elements as one of the top 25 places to eat in the country —and at number 20 in 2014. Geared to high-end fine dining, with tasting menus and wine pairings, its nine-course chefs menu focuses on local steak and seafood.

Dishes such as the popular 48-hour short rib—with pine nut, tomato, buckwheat, sweet potato, and ricotta—and Spanish mackerel —with rice cake, charred scallion, oyster mushroom, sesame, and ginger—are carefully tweaked to take full advantage of the best produce available.

"It's a spontaneous menu that evolves from day to day, as we work with the freshest ingredients that come in," says Scott.

Dining options

While elements offers an elegant formal setting for special occasions, Scott's second restaurant, Mistral, provides a more informal environment for everyday eating. If the dining experience is more relaxed, however, the kitchen's commitment to local and seasonal produce is no less serious.

Guests can choose from a range of small plates to share, from "the fields," "the water," or "the land." And although the ingredients are local, Scott employs cooking styles from around the world. "At Mistral, customers can sample fresh, lively dishes from Japan, Korea, Provence, the Basque Country, the Mediterranean, Mexico, and the best of America," he says. "It offers everything from kimchi pancakes to salt-and-pepper calamari, and whole-roasted quail to local tilefish and homemade charcuterie."

In both of his restaurants, Scott's passion for cooking and his preference for seasonal ingredients shine through. All meat—from hogs to poultry and game—is raised sustainably, and all ingredients are field fresh thanks to the great relationship he has with his neighboring farmers. So, whether they are sharing small plates with friends at Mistral or celebrating an anniversary at elements, guests know they are eating food that's fresh, flavorful, and never the same twice.

www.mistralprinceton.com

INDOMITABLE SPIRIT

*The Nolet family's deluxe gins and vodkas draw on
11 generations of tradition and expertise, distilling three
centuries of history into each bottle*

Tradition runs strong in the Nolet family. Every year on his birthday, Carolus Nolet Sr. announces the latest release of NOLET'S® Reserve Dry Gin. Fewer than 700 bottles of this exclusive spirit are produced a year, each of which costs $700, making it the world's most expensive gin. Flavored with precious saffron and verbena, it has been honed by Carolus over decades and has won multiple awards including a five-star rating from F. Paul Pacult in *The Spirit Journal*.

With nearly 325 years of distilling experience to its name, Nolet Distillery has been passed down from father to son for 11 generations. The family, which founded Nolet Distillery in 1691, prides itself on its history and craftsmanship while valuing innovation.

"With a family business, you have to look ahead," says 11th-generation family member Carl Nolet Jr. "My father, Carolus, always says 'history doesn't pay the bills.'" It was Carolus who challenged Carl Jr. and his brother Bob to create a contemporary fine gin different from anything else on the market. The result was NOLET'S Silver Dry Gin, which features a distinctive combination of botanicals including Turkish rose, peach, and raspberry. The creation of NOLET'S Finest Gins followed on from the success of the family's Ketel® One Vodka, of which more than two million cases are sold every year across 50 countries.

Distilled history

What sets NOLET'S apart from other brands is its unrivaled distilling process. The Nolet family, which employs 200 people worldwide, owns the oldest distillery in Schiedam, the city near Rotterdam, Holland that has been its base since 1691. The entire production process takes place under one roof using a specially commissioned copper still that combines pot still and column still distillation. Each botanical used is individually macerated and then distilled.

"We don't buy time at a bottling factory," says Carl Jr. "Our bespoke spirits don't leave the distillery until they are fully bottled. We are completely authentic." Consumers are invited to visit Nolet Distillery and experience for themselves exactly where the Nolets have been crafting spirits for more than three centuries.

There is one further tradition that Carolus and his sons always uphold. Before the spirits are bottled, a member of the family samples each batch. It's yet another example of how this family ensures its legacy will endure for many years to come.

www.noletsgin.com

DISTILLED PASSION

From its intricate production process to the hand-sculpture of each bottle, Tequila Clase Azul is a work of art made by the craftspeople of Mexico

If you're born in the state of Jalisco in western Mexico, then you're born with tequila in your blood. So says Arturo Lomeli, the master distiller, founder, and CEO of Tequila Clase Azul. "That is because the agave plant, from which all tequila is made, grows in abundance in this mountainous and coastal state," he says. "It makes tequila a key industry in the region."

This ultra-premium line of tequilas is produced in the town of Jesús María. This is one of the highest points in the Los Altos region—the highlands of the state of Jalisco—and the altitude lends unique flavor profiles to the tequila. "The highlands are cooler," says Arturo, "so the plant needs less water, and less water means that more sugar can be retained."

The distilling process is just as particular, using traditional methods and cooking the agave in old-fashioned stone ovens. It takes 72 hours, ensuring a smoother, more refined tequila. For Tequila Clase Azul, it is always about quality over quantity. "Some people measure success in terms of money," says Arturo. "We measure it in terms of our customers' happiness—and that comes from providing them with the highest quality."

Quality control

The firm's tequila is either bottled or aged to create four distinctive versions of the drink. Most recognizable is the blue-and-white Tequila Clase Azul Reposado bottle, aged for eight months and priced at around $100. There is also the Tequila Clase Azul Plata, which is not aged; the Clase Azul Añejo, which is aged for a further 25 months; and, finally, the cream of the crop, the Clase Azul Ultra, which is produced in batches of only 100 and aged in sherry caskets for five years.

"Our clientele extends to those connoisseurs who appreciate the very best," says Arturo. The bottle itself takes at least two weeks to create, and—because each one is individually handcrafted—no two are the same.

In 2013, Tequila Clase Azul released a limited-edition set of 15 exquisitely crafted pieces filled with 15-year tequila. This significant project draws from hundreds of years of wisdom and a deep passion for the magical stories that capture Mexico's spirits and soul. And, starting at around $30,000 a bottle, every cent of profit from it is poured into the company's charitable foundation, the Fundación con Causa Azul, which supports Mexican artisans so they can continue to work.

"Our mission statement is simple: to share happiness and to captivate the world through the magic of tequila," says Arturo. "We are doing this because we love what we do, and because we are proud of our Mexican heritage—it's in our blood."

www.claseazul.com

WINE, ALL MINE

The Wine Foundry, based in California's famous Napa Valley, gives enthusiasts the chance to craft custom wines of their very own

With degrees in fermentation science, Steve Ryan is ideally qualified to run The Wine Foundry. This unique winery, based in the famous wine-growing region of Napa Valley, California, gives people the opportunity to custom order their own premium wine, starting with an impressive selection of grapes from California's most prestigious vineyards.

Clients work with award-winning winemakers to achieve the desired attributes for an exceptional wine, while the design team assists with custom-designed labels and packaging.

DIY—with expert help

The Wine Foundry's experienced staff executes each detail at the highest level, right down to the stamp on the cork. Clients can participate in the winemaking as much as they choose, or they can leave everything to the winery's experienced pros. "Some people like to engage in every aspect of the process," says Steve, the firm's General Manager. "We love it when our clients visit and get involved."

With an international client list, the firm will also deliver samples and conduct virtual blending sessions with clients via Skype. "Our goal is to tailor a client's wine to their individual palate," says Head Winemaker Patrick Saboe, "creating the most enjoyable experience possible." The result is a rare creation of truly bespoke wine.

Clients find a variety of reasons to come to The Wine Foundry. "There are enthusiasts who want to create a signature wine for their own collection," says Steve. "There are corporations crafting customized wines as gifts for valued customers or employees. And there are groups of friends who want to learn about the process while making great wine together."

Very few wineries currently provide this experience. "Making highly customized, premium wines requires specialized skills and equipment," says Steve, "along with exceptional customer service." So well has the business been going that, in 2014, The Wine Foundry purchased new premises in Napa Valley.

"What we're doing is very innovative," says Patrick. "Most wineries make four or five different wines; we're doing 400 or 500 in small batches. We give people a gateway into creating their own wine. It's not just about wine—it's the pursuit of a passion and the realization of a dream."

www.thewinefoundry.com

Chapter 6
LUXURY LIVING

A PERFECT FIT

The long-term investment in quality that is a bespoke suit from Savile Row tailor Davies and Son in London is attracting an ever-widening international customer base

What connects Admiral Lord Nelson, Clark Gable, David Hockney, Bryan Ferry, Benny Goodman, and the Duke of Edinburgh? It's that they all share a taste for finely cut suits made by the London tailor, Davies and Son.

London is recognized as a world-leader in men's bespoke tailoring, with Savile Row at its center. Founded in 1803, Davies and Son is Savile Row's oldest established independent firm, its immaculate clothes renowned around the world.

After more than 200 years of impeccable service, the company is now in the safe hands of current owner and master tailor Alan Bennett (pictured opposite). Alan came to Savile Row as a 15-year-old apprentice and has since accumulated 49 years' worth of experience. In recognition of his services to the tailoring industry, he was made a Freeman of the City of London in 2005.

Military fit

Like many Savile Row tailors, Davies and Son was established as a military outfitters. Nelson soon became a client, and most of his officers duly also made the firm their tailor. At the time, the owner Thomas Davies boasted that he dressed "all the crowned heads of Europe."

Tailoring for the majority of today's clients, however, relies less on braid and buckles than on the more exacting art of cutting to flatter the figure. The cutter, who takes around five years to learn his craft, is the key figure at the beginning of the long process of turning measurements into a perfectly proportioned, exquisitely comfortable suit. It is the job of his colleagues to bring together the wool and mohair canvasses, the horsehair chest piece, fabric from a range of 2,000 samples, and linings.

The company also makes use of the finest British wools, cashmere and wool blends, linen and silk blends, and traditional Scottish tweeds. From the angle of the lapel, the set of the buttonholes, and the way pinstripes are cut

to meet at the shoulder seam, the bespoke process allows each client to specify the precise details of his suit.

Classic silhouette

There is, however, a classic Davies and Son silhouette into which these details are incorporated. "Our house style is a straight shoulder line with a high armhole for comfort and a small drape on the chest tapering to a subtle waist to flatter the client's shape," says Alan. This can be seen in a 1963 woollen suit made for the Duke of Windsor (pictured left, bottom), or in the tailored jackets that Davies and Son make for each individual member of the Bentley Owners Club (pictured left, top).

> "THE BESPOKE PROCESS ALLOWS EACH CLIENT TO SPECIFY THE PRECISE DETAILS OF HIS SUIT"

Accuracy at the cutting stage means overseas clients are not tied to the traditional three fittings often required to complete a suit. Instead, one fitting after measurements have been taken will generally suffice. This makes long-distance tailoring an option for the company's international clientele. And, with the USA as the firm's largest overseas market, the company makes four visits to seven major cities there every year. There are also trips to Norway, Japan, France, Germany, and Switzerland.

"Our business is evolving all the time," says Alan. "We are now in South Korea and see China as our next major market." Customers in a position to order at least eight suits at a time are guaranteed a visit by the team anywhere in the world.

Back in Central London, though many tailors share the same postcode as Davies and Son, Alan is adamant that they are worlds apart. "With us, you are getting a work of art," he says, "and a garment that will mould to your shape. It is timeless, like the tradition that made it."

www.daviesandson.com

PRELOVED LUXURY

Offering unprecedented, and instant, access to exclusive designer brands, Portero is the leading online marketplace for immaculate and authentic pre-owned luxury goods

Waiting is not something the rich and famous of this world often experience. Be it for restaurant tables, commercial flights, or the latest miracle face cream, money does not like to stand in line.

However, when the coveted item is a vintage luxury brand handbag, everyone waits. Not even royalty can simply walk into a shop and walk out with their design of choice.

"It doesn't matter who you are, or even if you have an open checkbook, you cannot go to a Hermès store, let's say, unannounced and leave with any bag you want," says Portero Director Alexis Clarbour. It is a market gap that Portero, the luxury secondary goods website, has been filling for more than a decade. Customers can detail the exact size, style, or color of the bag they are looking for and the company's concierge service will source it for them.

Eagle-eyed staff
The New York-based operation offers jewelry, watches, and accessories, too, though bags are its most popular sellers. Relatively rare luxury goods such as pre-owned Hermès and Chanel bags are often extremely valuable. "A Birkin's resale value can change quickly," says Alexis. "And certain colors are more valuable depending on the season and availability."

Portero's highly trained staff is eagle-eyed when it comes to spotting fakes. "We have a team of authenticators who check everything," says Alexis. "The 'Portero promise' is that if something is ever sold that is not completely authentic, we will refund the sale. It is becoming increasingly difficult to spot fakes—in particular 'super fakes,' which would take an expert to identify—but we are relentless and meticulous in doing so."

Pristine products
Portero began life 10 years ago as an eBay store selling a range of items including art, antiques, furs, and shoes. As it grew, it focused on its bestselling lines in order to offer only the best, with many items being completely unused. "I was adamant that we would only sell pristine or truly excellent pieces," says Alexis. "Quality and authenticity are of the utmost importance. We source those products you can't get in regular stores."

The vintage trend has also contributed to interest in the site. "That whole market is huge," says Alexis. "People understand value in a different way today. It is now extremely chic to go to a dinner party in vintage, whereas years ago it wasn't like that."

While Portero can offer an entry point into high-end goods for dedicated savers, its typical customer is well-off and female. "An average transaction is around $2,000 per order," says Alexis. "Our prices and selection are very hard to beat. We have Hollywood names, sportspeople, and royalty among our clientele. These people want what they want, when they want it. We are able to provide that instant gratification, with the standards expected of a luxury brand."

"QUALITY AND AUTHENTICITY ARE OF THE UTMOST IMPORTANCE"

Such a high level of customer service is just one of Portero's assets. "It is incredibly satisfying to be able to deliver exactly what a customer has asked for," says Alexis, "and on the day they asked for it, with no waiting required. To our customers, as well as to us, that is priceless."
www.portero.com

PICTURE PERFECT

New York photographer Lucille Khornak's family shoots capture whimsical moments and transform them into precious, soulful works of art

Photographer Lucille Khornak is in a contemplative mood. She is sitting in her gallery in the Hamptons, on New York's Long Island, against a backdrop of sculpted handbags and some of her own pieces. Why is it, she ponders, that people take so many photographs these days?

"Photography captures a moment we can never go back to," she says, "but it can trigger memories in the future."

For the last 20 years, Lucille has been triggering memories for some of America's best

and brightest. Having started off as a professional model, she went on to become a commercial photographer, employed by the likes of Denaka Vodka and Karl Lagerfeld Jewelry.

Then, in the mid-1990s, her mother became ill and she switched course. "Going between the hospital and photographing beautiful women in couture gowns grew increasingly difficult," she says. "The fashion just didn't seem real."

Lucille began picking up more satisfying work with clients such as Johnson & Johnson and Cheerios. Being around children gave her

energy. "I'd always wanted children, and the universe gave me lots of them on photo shoots," she says. "I'd get my fix of kids and then I'd get to go home at night!"

Moments of whimsy

Family photography quickly became her primary business. Lucille developed a style that captured beautiful family moments while incorporating her fine arts background.

"I like to take a whimsical moment and make it into an energetic, soulful piece of art," she says. "At one shoot in Mauritius, instead of everyone standing and posing, I captured them all with just their heads out of the water and the lights of the island reflecting around them. Another time, we found a tiny little frog and I got one of the kids to put it on his nose. I took the shot as the frog was falling off and the boy was trying to catch it."

There is no standard approach for Lucille when it comes to a photo shoot, no "tricks" that she keeps up her sleeve. "All I ask is for clients to come prepared for some fun," she says. Considering the number of clients that book Lucille for yearly appointments, she must be onto something.

"I come from the point of view that family photos should be treated as art in the home," says Lucille. She offers custom hardcover books and also the bespoke design of a picture wall in a client's home.

"We don't turn anything out unless it's quality," she says. "We deal with quality people and they deserve the best."
www.lucillekhornak.com

STEP OUT IN STYLE

Back At The Ranch's handmade cowboy boots aren't just true American classics—they're also a mighty fine investment

The cowboy boot is an American design classic, along with blue jeans and Chevrolet cars. However, it takes an experienced craftsman to create the genuine item, which is why Back At The Ranch only picks those with years of experience.

"We work with an extended family of second- and third-generation craftsmen," says owner Wendy Henry. "These are men who have spent their lives making cowboy boots, each one by hand, at our factory in El Paso, Texas. It's a dying art and it's passed down over the years—we're keeping these unrivaled skills alive."

As one of the last makers of bespoke cowboy boots, Back At The Ranch focuses on luxury and quality, and produces only a limited number of boots a year. Wendy and her team are expert at creating designs that meet the individual demands and tastes of customers, consulting with them on color, stitching, and fit. From ostrich to alligator, there's no limit to the range of exotic and rare skins they can choose from—and customers can even select the exact section of hide from which they want their design made.

Statement boots
The finished result, embellished with hand-created patterns, is a work of art, and lends the wearer a presence that, says Wendy, no ordinary boot can. "It's about an attitude," she says. "It changes your bearing when you put on a cowboy boot because they fit differently from a shoe. If you really need to let the world know who you are, then our boots will do that."

For many, a pair of Back At The Ranch boots is an investment. Mothers will buy them for both themselves and their children. Politicians buy them, as do country and western stars, and Hollywood actors. Founded in 1990, this Santa Fe, New Mexico-based retailer also has a global clientele. In addition to classic designs, Wendy has introduced on-trend creations such as footwear with all-purpose Vibram soles, and customers can personalize their boots. Back At The Ranch also stocks handmade pairs in a range of sizes online and in store.

The secret to the success of Back At The Ranch lies in the company's motto: "Perfection is in the details." Durable and crafted down to the last stitch, these timeless American classics are guaranteed never to walk out of style.
www.backattheranch.com

SPOTLESS GRANDEUR

*Clients from New York and around the world entrust
The Madame Paulette Organization to clean, repair,
and restore their antique couture and treasured artifacts*

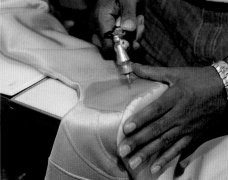

The fabric of life passes through the doors of Madame Paulette's Manhattan flagship boutique every day. Stories are woven into each one of the vintage furs, couture suits, intricate bridal gowns, and crisp businessmen's shirts that the cleaners transform and repair using their specialist care and attention to detail. With a team of trained craftsmen and artisans there's little that the staff at Madame Paulette can't renew, making it one of the world's leading cleaning and restoration specialists.

New York is not the only place to benefit from Madame Paulette's services. As specialists in their field, Madame Paulette's team of professionals have cleaned Parisian couture, vintage uniforms of British prime ministers, and even valeted a private plane belonging to Donald Trump several times.

"We're performing miracles day after day," says John Mahdessian, President of this third-generation, family-owned institution. "I believe we're the only place in the world that can fix what's considered unsalvageable."

Creative restoration

As well as cleaning delicate, vintage couture, the team of tailors and dressmakers can replace entire panels, re-bead antique evening gowns, and restore vintage military uniforms. They even contact craftspeople who can duplicate old buttons and re-dye any fabric to match exactly. "Our specialists are consistently coming up with creative solutions," says John, "to rebuild, re-dye, and restore items for anyone across the globe."

For 55 years Madame Paulette has continued to develop its state-of-the-art techniques. "It's why people entrust us with their most special possessions," says John. The company's global, discerning clientele includes billionaires and CEOs, museums and galleries, and acclaimed fashion designers, including Louis Vuitton, Vera Wang, and Oscar de la Renta. In addition, a destination valet brings the fine services of Madame Paulette to clients across the US, organizing the collection of clothes and luggage, cleaning and pressing them, and sending them on to the next destination.

"We can even offer advice to anyone around the globe via email," says John. Indeed, clients can send digital images of their most treasured pieces to the New York offices and have a full evaluation thanks to the varied experience of Madame Paulette's cleaning and restoration specialists.

If the fabric of life has a stain, some will fret. But now, with Madame Paulette, a loved garment, an antique chair, or even a luxury car in need of restoration can be returned to its original splendor.

www.madamepaulette.com

SAFE AND SOUND

Whether it's supplying private bodyguards, policing events, or providing self-defense training, Houston's UPI Security is all about delivering a high-quality service and peace of mind

When Tony Skinner decided to set up the security firm Ultra Protection Inc (UPI) a decade ago, he knew that he'd be putting himself in a position of danger. "I've always wanted to be someone's hero," says Tony. "Everything I've done in my career has been about seizing the opportunity to be that."

Consequently, Tony is the guy you want covering your back. A former police officer, he dedicated nine years of his life to the military and became a martial arts expert before launching UPI in Houston in 2004. Today, the company offers a range of services—from event security to self-defense training—while its heartland remains providing private protection. "When people ask me what I do, I say I protect people that can't otherwise protect themselves," says Tony. "I take great pride in being able to do that."

The company's service and standards are, therefore, exceptionally high. "From day one, I've looked at the government requirements in terms of training and standards, and I've set to blow them out of the water," says Tony. "It means that UPI surpasses the state standards for security officers by three times or more."

Raising the bar

His philosophy is simple: because UPI demands unparalleled training and dedication, it pays more than other private security firms. This enables Tony to acquire some of the most qualified officers and offer a personalized, premium service.

"Our clients are looking for people they trust; people who know what they're doing." And Tony personally ensures that this is exactly what they receive.

As a result, his client list includes high-profile names such as the Houston Rockets basketball star Tracy McGrady, *Nip/Tuck* actress Jennifer Sciole, and senior executives of several major oil, gas, and energy companies. "There's not a single contract that I haven't personally negotiated," says Tony.

Yet, while such a personalized service sets UPI apart, its founder's passion and dedication also play their part. "This is more than a career for me," says Tony. "It's my place in life." It also affords him the chance to be heroic on a daily basis. But, perhaps more importantly, as he puts it, "It's a noble profession. There's honor in what I do."

www.upisecurity.com

Chapter 7
STYLISH ESTATES

ROOMS WITH A VIEW

Luxury property specialist the Private Client Group at Russ Lyon Sotheby's International Realty delivers local knowledge, a global network, and spectacular panoramas

A good view, it seems, sells a property in Arizona: whether it's of the mountains, a golf course, or the city lights. Before considering room sizes or carports, potential homeowners are mentally breathing in the warm desert air, gazing at the starry sky, and admiring the way the mountains rise above a vista of manicured golfing greens.

"CLIENTS GRAVITATE TO US BECAUSE OF OUR PROFICIENCY AND GLOBAL OUTREACH. THEY KNOW WE ARE DISCREET, SAVVY, AND WELCOMING"

Competition for a dream home in sought-after areas such as Scottsdale and Paradise Valley is intense and requires a realtor with superior local knowledge and international contacts. This is why the Private Client Group at Russ Lyon Sotheby's International Realty, one of the largest of the Sotheby's International franchises, has grown so successfully and offers an exceptional portfolio that includes estates costing up to around $35 million.

"Jobs follow people, so executives and entrepreneurs moving to Arizona for the lifestyle have brought greater business opportunities to the area," says Frank Aazami, owner of the Private Client Group. "I founded the company in 2007 to provide a discreet, professional service with these high-profile figures in mind."

Smarter cities

Entrepreneurs can instantly recognize a good investment. And as a young state, Arizona boasts well designed housing and city infrastructures. Indeed, easily navigable grid systems divide residential from industrialized areas. "There are buffers in place to separate residences from commercialized areas," says Frank, "so beyond your area of work, you can easily find tranquil, artfully designed residential communities."

The Private Client Group's current team of sales associates has been working together for around eight years. "Clients gravitate to us because of our proficiency and global outreach," says Frank. "They know we are discreet, savvy, and welcoming. They want to tell us their stories. It's like the old-fashioned way when your realtor was a lifelong partner that your parents used, you used, then your kids used."

With a wide range of architectural styles to choose from, such as Santa Fe, Tuscan, Ranch, and Contemporary, of different sizes and prices, Frank and the elite Private Client Group team can offer clients detailed search options to tailor their inquiry. The Private Client Group website allows clients to specify their tastes down to details such as a preference for granite work surfaces or open fireplaces. "In addition," says Frank, "we showcase every home's story through video and text, using a local production company and writers."

A global client base

Working with Sotheby's International Realty expands the Private Client Group's reach across Europe and Asia, giving Frank's property portfolio the widest audience possible. "It's about how many buyers you can feature your property in front of," he says. "You can't sell a secret."

Overseas clients, as well as those from across America, many of whom own multiple properties, benefit from the Private Client Group's creative financing options. These might include the seller acting as the lender, using collectibles and high-value goods as part of the trade, or the buyer and seller entering into a lease and purchase agreement together. Clients dictate if they prefer these financing options or not; the majority do not, but it provides another tool to consider.

One thing it is hard to put a price on is quality of life. Perhaps ironically, with many luxury properties on his books at any one time, Frank himself rarely has time to stand around taking in the view.

www.privateclientgroupagents.com

BEACHSIDE LUXURY

The Estates at Acqualina in sun-drenched Florida
aren't just opulent resorts—they are homes where couples
and families will want to live

It was only built in 2006, but the five-star Acqualina Resort & Spa on the Beach has quickly become one of Miami's go-to resorts. Towering 51 stories high over Sunny Isles Beach, the hotel has received numerous accolades, including a top rating from Forbes Travel Guide and the AAA Five Diamond Award. Also in the company's impressive repertoire is The Mansions at Acqualina—based south of the Acqualina Resort & Spa, these unprecedented sky mansions redefine luxury living.

Following on from the popular demand created by both the Resort & Spa and The Mansions, Acqualina is now building The Estates at Acqualina, comprising two luxury residential towers within a gated community. 777 Acqualina Place will offer exquisite half- and full-floor residences ranging from 4,465 to just over 5,000 sq ft, as well as a single family home, a tower suite and a two-story Penthouse Estate— all with private leisure pools. 888 Acqualina Place, on the other hand, will offer luxurious residences that range in size from 2,800 to 3,665 sq ft.

"There was huge interest from people looking for larger residential units that had Acqualina's five-star amenities and lifestyle," says Michael Goldstein, President of Sales at Acqualina.

The Estates' two graceful towers will boast breathtaking views of the Atlantic Ocean. "The floor plans are very spacious and 'flow-thru,'" says Michael. "Each private terrace will have an outdoor spa, sauna and summer kitchen, making this one of the few buildings in South Florida where you can barbecue on the balcony."

Ready for living

Inside, residents will find spacious en-suites, his-and-hers dressing rooms, and a sumptuously appointed kitchen. One of the outstanding features of The Estates is that owners will be able to move straight in, as each residence will come "furniture ready." The interiors will have an impressive selection of finishes, with onyx countertops and marble floors throughout.

The utmost care will be taken of these homes when residents are away, with housekeeping restocking fridges and arranging fresh flowers in time for the owners' return for a fee, while a Rolls-Royce house car will always be on stand-by.

"PEOPLE DON'T JUST COME TO FLORIDA FOR A VACATION—THEY COME HERE TO LIVE"

The centerpiece of this new development will be a spectacular, multi-million dollar Mediterranean-style villa complex, designed by the renowned architect Rafael Portuondo. Located between the towers, it is emblematic of the luxurious and exclusive world created by Acqualina. Surrounded by acres of lush landscaped gardens, six pools, and a romantic beachfront restaurant and bar, Villa Acqualina will offer more than 45,000 sq ft of remarkable amenities. These include the villa's Circus Maximus, a full floor of extraordinary facilities such as an ice skating rink, bowling lanes and a movie theater. It also boasts a Wall Street Trader's

Club room, while budding surfers can catch some waves on a FlowRider® on Acqualina's beach.

A family affair

"People don't just come to Florida for a vacation," says Michael. "They come here to live." And with six swimming pools, a game room, and a kids' arcade, The Estates and the nearby Acqualina Resort & Spa are also very family orientated.

"With an expanding portfolio of larger-than-life resort-style amenities, The Estates will bring an exciting, new, action-packed lifestyle to South Florida," adds Michael. "Following on from the sell-out of The Mansions, we're confident The Estates will appeal to buyers interested in an incomparable level of opulence."

From unrivaled indoor and outdoor amenities and estate-sized residences with sweeping Atlantic Ocean views to five-star hotel-style services, residents will enjoy a lifestyle beyond compare. The Estates at Acqualina offers Miami's most exquisite beachfront living experience, and is poised to change the Miami skyline forever.

www.estatesatacqualina.com

THE REAL DEAL

Boasting a passion for real estate that spans 15 years,
Connecticut-based realtor Barbara Brock Zaccagnini uses
her inside expertise to find customers their ideal home

An associate of international brokerage Coldwell Banker, Barbara is recognized as one of the leading realtors in Greenwich, Connecticut. One of her strengths is her ability to work with a diverse range of clients—from CEOs and celebrities to first-time buyers—and always with characteristic discretion.

Insider knowledge

A resident herself for more than 30 years, Barbara chose Greenwich for its proximity to beaches and backcountry woodland, as well as it being just 38 minutes by train from Manhattan's Grand Central Station. Her in-depth, insider knowledge comes from more than 15 years' experience in the local property industry, and Barbara is also licensed in both Connecticut and New York. "Greenwich, Fairfield County, and neighboring Westchester County offer clean, beautiful towns that are home to affluent communities and good schools," says Barbara. "Properties hold their value, and the people are friendly and genuinely care about their communities."

Greenwich offers downtown living as well as backcountry acreage, and locales like Meads Point and Belle Haven that are characterized by large waterfront properties in gated communities. Greenwich itself boasts all the amenities and cultural attractions of a medium-sized city—including the much-loved Bruce Museum—as well as parks, beaches, and views of Long Island Sound.

Informed instinct

Barbara's creative approach to marketing exploits a wide range of tools—from online listings to targeted publications—and her expert staging ensures properties are always displayed at their best. Her relationship with Coldwell Banker means her clients benefit from the resources and connections of a major international company, at a time when Greenwich is experiencing an influx of international buyers.

"The market is continually changing," says Barbara, "so I make it my business to know everything I can that would benefit my clients."

For Barbara Brock Zaccagnini, a career in real estate is more than just selling property—it's about developing a relationship with her clients. It is this that makes finding the perfect home possible.

"I feel enthusiastic every time I'm involved with a new client," she says. "I make sure to give the client as much time and energy as it takes to find exactly what they are looking for."

A winner of Coldwell Banker's International Premier's Award in multiple years—most recently in 2014—Barbara has been a top associate since joining Coldwell Banker in 2007. Key to this success is the time she takes to understand every client's needs, whether they are local or international buyers.

"I like to spend time with my clients first," she says, "not just to learn what they're looking for in a home, but to clearly recognize their lifestyle and hear their needs."

> "I USE AN INFORMED INSTINCT TO BUY OR SELL A HOME THAT WORKS PERFECTLY FOR EACH INDIVIDUAL"

For some clients, this careful attention leads them to something they didn't know they wanted. "I'll meet a client who thinks they want new, and then they end up buying an older home," she says. "I use an informed instinct to buy or sell a home that works perfectly for each individual."

By combining her extensive knowledge of Greenwich and its surrounds with a genuine commitment to understanding her clients' needs, Barbara has cemented a reputation for excellence. "It's not just about selling homes," she says. "It's about providing a superior and personal relationship based on service—because that's how you sell or find the perfect home for someone." *www.4homesbybarbara.com*

MAGIC IN RESIDENCE

Homeowners can live the dream at Golden Oak at
Walt Disney World Resort, which offers luxury homes
just four miles from Magic Kingdom Park

A trip to Disney World holds magical memories for children and adults alike. Now, enthusiasts can go one step further—they can actually live at Walt Disney World Resort, close to the world-famous theme parks.

Located just four miles from Magic Kingdom Park, Golden Oak at Walt Disney World Resort is a luxury residential resort community of single-family custom homes. This 980-acre gated community in Florida—set in a conservation area—is the first to offer private homes at Walt Disney World Resort. Page Pierce, Vice President of Disney Resort Real Estate Development, says that the artfully designed, custom-built homes allow families to enjoy a luxury resort lifestyle all year round.

"For people who've grown up visiting our theme parks, Golden Oak provides the chance to live here," he says. "It's a magical place for residents to create lasting memories and traditions for generations to come."

All-access living

There is no doubting the unique access that comes with being a Golden Oak resident. Summerhouse, the community's 17,000-sq ft clubhouse, is available exclusively for residents, and features such amenities as a heated outdoor pool, a fitness center, the full-service Markham's dining room, and Tyler's Lounge.

The club's Resident Services team is dedicated to providing concierge-style services, including dining and spa reservations, park transportation and tickets, golf services, and more. They can also assist in planning and creating events such as dessert parties in the club and theme parks.

"We pride ourselves on providing an impeccable service, one that ensures our residents enjoy effortless and unforgettable experiences," says Page. "It's just one of many perks that comes with living at Walt Disney World Resort."

Personalized attention

Many of the homes boast pools, courtyards, and guest houses. All must meet the highest design and build standards. In order to do so, the master plan for Golden Oak includes an extensive architectural styles book inspired by old-world Mediterranean and Caribbean architecture with Venetian, Dutch, and Tuscan design influences. Although residents can design the interiors as they please, the exterior architecture must be historically accurate and tasteful. "Authenticity and quality are important to us, so nothing can be faux or veneer on the outside of the homes," says Page.

> "WE PROVIDE AN IMPECCABLE SERVICE—ONE THAT ENSURES OUR RESIDENTS ENJOY EFFORTLESS, UNFORGETTABLE EXPERIENCES"

Buyers work directly with one of seven carefully selected, premier custom homebuilders from Central Florida to create their ideal residence. Additionally, the owner oversees construction to guarantee quality and personalized attention.

The appeal of Golden Oak at Walt Disney World Resort is international, with buyers coming from as far as the UK and China, as well as the USA. And it is not just Disney aficionados that are attracted to the resort community.

"Our buyers love Disney but you don't have to be an enthusiast to appreciate our unique offering," says Page. "It's about fine living in the most magical place, having fun with your family and loved ones, and creating everlasting memories." A haven indeed for those who are still young at heart.
www.disneygoldenoak.com

A MATTER OF COURSE

*Georgia-based Hilda W. Allen Real Estate Inc. has
firmly established itself as one of the big hitters in the
world of golf real-estate*

For nearly 30 years, Hilda W. Allen has specialized in golf and resort real-estate—her mix of expertise and tenacity establishing her as one of America's leading figures in the industry. In 2014, Hilda's pioneering work in selling golf courses at auction earned her a place in the Georgia Auctioneer Hall of Fame, making her the first female to receive this honor.

Since Hilda W. Allen Real Estate Inc. was established in 1991, Hilda has sold more than 800 golf courses, representing sales worth over $875 million. "It's my passion," she says. "It is perhaps why I've been so successful in an often male-dominated business. One of my customers told me 'You take no prisoners!'"

Accelerated sales

Even when they're changing hands, golf courses need to keep operating. "It's difficult to sell an ongoing business without it causing disruption," says Hilda. It's why her company specializes in accelerated sales, where potential buyers bid competitively to establish a true market price. "Prices and bids are confidential," says Hilda. "This approach creates a sense of urgency among buyers, putting the seller in control."

Using an accelerated sales method can make the sale move quicker and more smoothly, and the entire process normally takes around 90 days. Because all due diligence is completed before the date of the sale, the potential for last-minute problems is minimized.

Hilda offers a range of accelerated sales methods, including the absolute sale, where the property title must pass to the highest bidder, and the reserve sale, where the title must pass to the highest bidder above an undisclosed reserve bid established by the seller before the auction. She has also developed her own signature method, the hybrid sealed-bid offering, where top bidders participate in one final bidding round at the seller's option.

An international affair

Hilda W. Allen Real Estate is a global business that represents clients from around the world, ranging from doctors and lawyers to businessmen and large corporations. Hilda's reputation means that she has built up a loyal client base that returns again and again. "I've got a lot of repeat business from buyers and sellers," she says. "A lot of the buyers have bought five or six golf courses. The loyalty of my customers is probably my proudest achievement. Being selected to buy or sell based on past business is a real honor."

> ## "THE LOYALTY OF MY CUSTOMERS IS PROBABLY MY PROUDEST ACHIEVEMENT"

It is not just her clients who recognize that Hilda is exceptionally good at what she does. She is also acclaimed by her peers. In 2001, Hilda became the first female president of the Georgia Auctioneers Association. On admitting her to its Hall of Fame in 2014, the association described Hilda as a "pioneer" who has "worked hard to gain respect in a male-dominated profession." They praised her values of "human contact, personal interaction, and education of buyers and sellers."

Hilda has also won *The BoardRoom* magazine's Excellence in Achievement award for Real Estate Services of the Year three years in a row—in 2012, 2013, and again in 2014. The magazine caters to board members of private clubs, and recipients of its awards are selected by industry experts and peers.

Over her long and illustrious career in golf real-estate, Hilda has established a leading position in the industry. And her passion, tenacity, and pioneering approach have earned her the esteem of clients and peers alike.

www.hildawallen.com

HEART AND HEARTH

For the Ontario-based luxury realty brokerage
The Invidiata Team, a successful business is built
on the heartfelt principles of love, trust, and respect

The key to success in business, without question, is to love your customers, says Christopher Invidiata, owner of The Invidiata Team—a luxury real-estate company based in Oakville, Ontario. "Genuine love," he says, "is the most powerful thing on the planet."

It's an ethos that Christopher applies wholeheartedly to his company. Founded in 1985, The Invidiata Team is now a family business, with Christopher at the helm supported by his daughter, Shae, and son, Caleb.

"Our philosophy is very simple," explains Christopher, referencing a book entitled *The Greatest Salesman in the World*. "It tells the story of a little boy. Every person he met, he would tell them—without words—that he loved them. He became the most trusted merchant in the Middle East, known for his honesty."

An intimate business

This spirit of love, observes Christopher, is the heartbeat of The Invidiata Team. "We love one another and appreciate the uniqueness of every client," he says. "When someone invites you to market their home, you become involved in a very intimate part of their life. They may be getting divorced or have failed in business—or they may be moving up in the world, or need a bigger place for a new baby. When I sell a home, the gratitude and trust that you get from the homeowner is an intangible experience. It is truly a gift."

Christopher learned this early on and grew his business—and his reputation—by paying back in kind. "I wanted to thank clients for their business, and took them out to celebrate," he says. "Going for dinners with clients blossomed new friendships, which grew into lifelong relationships. These friends then began to refer and introduce me to their own circles. It was a very organic process of development."

Head start

Underlying this compassion and generosity is wisdom. "I grew my business on knowledge," says Christopher. "We have accurate, detailed records of real estate, and we offer those insights with impeccable service."

"WHEN SOMEONE INVITES YOU TO MARKET THEIR HOME, YOU BECOME INVOLVED IN A VERY INTIMATE PART OF THEIR LIFE"

What Christopher calls "the surprise and delights" come as extras. The thank-you dinners, the beautiful flowers when a client lists their home, the wine and gifts when they sell, and the subsequent gestures of appreciation. "Through all of this, we become an experiential group, not just limited to real estate." The Invidiata Team also prides itself on its creative thinking and a desire to work with like-minded people. It publishes

a quarterly magazine, *The Invidiata Collection*, which is proudly associated with global companies like The Fairmont Hotels & Resorts. In addition, The Invidiata Team won the "#1 Team In The World" by RE/MAX International in 2007 and 2012; and sits on the exclusive Board Of Regents that governs Who's Who in Luxury Real Estate, the world's largest luxury realty network.

Christopher also places great importance on giving back to the community, both locally and globally. He supports a number of charities including Children's Miracle Network, SickKids Foundation, and The Red Cross, and the company has close links to Shae Invidiata's charity [free-them], which fights human trafficking.

"What we represent is a heartfelt passion to serve people," says Christopher. "It's never just about the end product—it's always about the nuances of care and compassion along the way." In short, it's about love.
www.invidiata.com

LAVISH LIVING

Josie Tong and her team at Sotheby's International Realty —Beverly Hills use their expertise to help overseas buyers negotiate the complex Los Angeles property market

Chinese investment in Los Angeles real estate is booming. In the USA alone it was reported to have hit $15 billion in 2014, with the city ranking second among US markets.

With 20 years' experience in consulting and management with multinational corporations, a decade's experience in the city's luxury real estate market, as well as being fluent in both Cantonese and Mandarin, Josie Tong at Sotheby's International Realty—Beverly Hills is perfectly positioned to cater for this growing number of international property investors.

International network

As a member of the world-renowned Sotheby's International Realty, Josie has an expansive international reach.

"I've been able to take advantage of the ever-growing global network of offices that are affiliated with Sotheby's International Realty," says Josie. "In the past year, I've attended auctions in New York City and Hong Kong, spoken at a global networking event, attended the grand opening of our Beijing office, and met with colleagues from all over the world. We regularly refer business to each other, collaboratively serving our clients' global real estate needs."

Clients come from all over the world, including Australia, Croatia, and the UK, but it is the Chinese customer base that is growing most dramatically. Josie and her multilingual team are helping to assist this rising demand. "Being able to converse with foreign clients in their native tongues helps to develop trust and understanding," she says. "It means the process is made easier for them, providing greater levels of transparency."

Josie and her team are known for their warmth, hard work, and professionalism. They take a personal approach to each client they work with, making the process bespoke according to particular needs. "When representing buyers, we not only try to find them the right house, but also introduce them to our extensive network of friends and advisers to help them settle into their new environment," says Josie. "We are not just selling a house, we are helping people realize a dream, a lifestyle, and a new life in an adopted country."

For sellers, the team are able to promote listings internationally and target niche markets for potential buyers—who are, in turn, reached via an array of extensive and carefully laid-out marketing plans.

"WE HELP PEOPLE REALIZE A DREAM, A LIFESTYLE, AND A NEW LIFE IN AN ADOPTED COUNTRY"

Community leadership

Josie is also actively involved in the wider L.A. community. She is serving as secretary on the board of the American Red Cross Santa Monica Bay chapter and is a member of the American Red Cross Tiffany Circle—a group of female leaders and philanthropists committed to the work of the Red Cross.

She also recently joined the Pacific Council on International Policy, an invitation-only organization committed to building the vast potential of the West Coast for impact on global issues, discourse, and policy.

Josie's unique blend of personal and professional skills, combined with an in-depth knowledge of the L.A. real estate market and an internationally connected team, has made her the Realtor® of choice for connecting buyers and sellers globally in the Los Angeles real estate market. It is this particular expertise that helps Josie deliver a much-needed service in what is a booming market.

www.relocatela.com

OCEANFRONT PARADISE

Sailfish Point Realty is the on-site broker for an exclusive,
member-owned community of luxurious residences and
amenities on Florida's idyllic Hutchinson Island

"THE NATURAL BEAUTY OF THE ISLAND IS ASTOUNDING. IT'S LUSHLY
LANDSCAPED AND SURROUNDED BY MILES OF PRISTINE BEACHES"

Florida's Sailfish Point is home to an exclusive community. "Anyone buying a property here will be welcomed by like-minded people," says Kristen Cheskaty, Managing Partner of Sailfish Point Realty, which acts as the on-site broker for the community's luxury properties. "They're open, friendly, and unpretentious, and new members are overwhelmed by the welcome they receive."

These new members are just as likely to be overwhelmed by the location of their purchase. Sitting on the southern peninsula of Florida's Hutchinson Island, the luxurious gated community is almost completely surrounded by natural waterways. Just 65 miles from the Bahamas, Sailfish Point has easy access to deep water and sports fishing, and has a 77-slip private marina that can accommodate vessels of up to 125 ft. It is also the only place in Florida from which it is possible to travel from the east to the west coast entirely via inland waterways.

"The natural beauty of the island is astounding," says Kristen. "It's lushly landscaped and surrounded by miles of pristine beaches. The ocean is a beautiful turquoise color; the beaches are sandy and white—it takes your breath away."

Luxury living

With just 520 residences on 532 acres, Sailfish Point offers a wide selection of exclusive and private properties. These range from luxury apartments and waterfront villas, to estate homes of up to 20,000 sq ft. "Once in a while, one of these properties will be come available to lease during the season—usually for people who want to live here but have yet to find the right property," says Kristen. "More often than not, by the end of that season they're proud homeowners."

This is hardly surprising. Sailfish Point also boasts a world-class Jack Nicklaus-designed 18-hole golf course, eight Har-Tru tennis courts for both night and day play, a full-service spa and fitness center, and a 60,000 sq ft Oceanfront Clubhouse. Casual dining can be enjoyed at the Beach Club, the Cross Roads Café, and the Marina Café, whereas the Ocean Room offers a more formal dining experience. And Sailfish Point's highly acclaimed wine list received the Club Managers Association of America's Award of Distinction in 2013, 2014, and 2015.

Thriving community

The nearby city of Stuart is quaint and thriving, and was previously named America's Most Beautiful City by the America in Bloom competition. Home to a range of boutiques, restaurants, and the historic Lyric Theatre, the city also hosts various festivals, such as the Stuart Air Show and the Christmas Boat Parade. But, with four international airports in close proximity, a private jet port just 10 minutes away, and a private helipad at Sailfish Point, the rest of the world is also incredibly easy to access.

For those staying in Florida, Sailfish Point offers a secure environment. With just one road leading in and out of the community, safety is maintained by a discreet security team—all of whom are first responders. And as a way of giving back to those who work in their oceanfront community, residents established the Sailfish Point Foundation in 1999 to assist staff members and their children with educational expenses. To date, the foundation has funded more than a 1,000 scholarships.

"It's a unique community in an idyllic setting," says Kristen. "It's why we're so proud to represent the beautiful properties at Sailfish Point, using our long-standing reputation for excellence, unparalleled local-market expertise, and genuine love of the location."

www.sailfishpoint.com

STAR-QUALITY RETREATS

*Luxury property brokerage Snell Real Estate employs decades
of experience to locate ideal homes in Los Cabos, Mexico—
a year-round destination for celebrities and families alike*

> "OUR CLIENTS ARE INVESTING IN A LIFESTYLE AND THE OPPORTUNITY TO CREATE EVERLASTING MEMORIES WITH THEIR FRIENDS AND FAMILY"

the area's top-selling real-estate brokerage, specializing in its finest properties.

It's not difficult to understand why stars such as Leonardo DiCaprio, George Clooney, and Cindy Crawford have become familiar faces in this chic, second-home resort destination. Along with stunning blue flag-rated beaches, the area boasts the finest spas, five-star restaurants, award-winning golf and water sports, and outstanding natural surroundings.

Growing appeal

"Los Cabos is a unique gem and an idyllic retreat," says Vanessa Fukunaga, Snell Real Estate President and CEO. "It is a destination that is being discovered by more and more people every year, thanks in part to the Hollywood crowd and in part to the accessibility provided by the internet." It is also a favorite destination for entrepreneurs and executives from across the globe.

"Focusing on real estate in the Los Cabos area has proven to be a wise investment strategy, supported by the strength of the economy throughout Mexico," adds Vanessa. "Clients of Snell Real Estate are not simply buying four walls and a roof, but rather they're investing in a lifestyle and the opportunity to create everlasting memories in paradise with their friends and family."

Indeed, Snell Real Estate represents some of the most exclusive, master-planned communities in Mexico. These include Chileno Bay, featuring a private, award-winning Tom Fazio-designed golf course, the one-of-a-kind complex of Mar Adentro, and the oceanside community of Puerto Los Cabos. More than 90 percent of all luxury properties are, in fact, listed and sold through Snell Real Estate, with prices starting at under $1 million and ranging up to $20 million.

Client community

With a team of more than 50 people, Snell Real Estate is the largest independent luxury brokerage in all of Baja California Sur. It is little surprise, therefore, that most buyers and sellers in the area choose Snell Real Estate.

The bedrock of the company is its sales force, and Vanessa takes great pride in the strong relationships the team forms with clients. "Our expert team of agents choose to live and work in this paradise, and are naturally very passionate about it," says Vanessa. "They are involved in community and philanthropic endeavors, and build long-lasting relationships throughout Los Cabos and beyond."

Using their passion for the destination as inspiration, Vanessa and her partners have also created *Ocean Blue*, a high-end luxury lifestyle magazine that is distributed throughout Baja, North America, Europe, and Asia. As well as promoting Los Cabos, *Ocean Blue* seamlessly embodies international style.

Such a passion is understandable, because when it comes to finding a lifestyle that combines luxury, sports, entertainment, and natural beauty, Los Cabos is a location that is hard to beat. And Snell Real Estate is the brokerage to find the perfect high-end home in this Mexican paradise.

www.snellrealestate.com

Los Cabos, located on the southern tip of Mexico's Baja California Peninsula, is renowned as a vacation hot spot for the Hollywood A-list, lured by a lifestyle of laid-back luxury amid breathtaking surroundings.

For those seeking their own dream home in this slice of paradise, which averages 350 days of sun per year, Snell Real Estate is

SAN FRANCISCO'S FINEST

*The Callan Real Estate Team provides those seeking
to purchase luxury properties in San Francisco with
unparalleled service and expertise*

San Francisco's luxury real-estate market pitches relentless demand against a concentrated stock of highly desirable, fast-selling properties. The inside track is everything, and Barbara Callan and her son Robert R. Callan Jnr. from McGuire Real Estate—fourth- and fifth-generation San Franciscans, respectively—are the city's number one real estate team, based on sales to date of more than $2.5 billion.

Together, they have an unrivaled knowledge of the San Francisco market, and have represented Warren Buffett, many well-known athletes, politicians and those in the worlds of business and entertainment. "We have high enthusiasm," says Barbara, "and we love what we do."

The core of the firm's business, between 85 and 90 percent, is through client referrals. "We are very hands-on and don't use assistants to take our viewings," says Robert. "Both my mother and I are there with a client throughout a transaction, and we continue our relationship beyond that transaction. Working effectively with the world's wealthiest and most discerning buyers and sellers is the core of our business. We strive for the whole experience to be as seamless and enjoyable as possible for everyone involved."

Early viewings
People often begin working with the Callans because they offer "pocket listings," which gives buyers the opportunity to offer on properties before they are entered into the open market. The Callans also provide the level of service that the luxury buyer understands and expects.

"We absolutely go above and beyond to get the best transaction for our clients, whether they are buying or selling," says Robert. "Our concierge service will handle every need from the beginning of the process to the end and beyond. We take very good care of all our client needs, including designers, architects, builders, gardeners, painters, stagers, housekeepers, and much more. Providing this service to our clients is crucial."

Buyers and sellers from around the world come to Barbara and Robert for up-to-the-minute market analysis of San Francisco. While the city is at the heart of the Callans' business, Robert makes regular trips to key real-estate markets such as Hong Kong and Shanghai. "These trips help us build and strengthen our business overseas and we learn how to do business effectively in those markets," he says. "We are able to better understand the culture of our international buyers coming here; how they communicate and how they negotiate."

Community connections
Being native San Franciscans goes deeper for the Callans than the local expertise they offer. "We are very entrenched in community life," says Barbara. She and Robert mentor new agents, and speak at colleges, young professional events, and major conferences. They are also actively involved in the Cancer Prevention Institute of California, while Barbara, with her family, works with The Link Fund, which raises around $1 million annually through the Plumpjack/Link Golf Classic. Robert also serves on the executive cabinet of the San Francisco Child Abuse Prevention Center.

"We are very involved in city life, but our clients know that we are always available for them," says Barbara. "Service to our clients is vital. Whether a client is buying or selling, is a first-time buyer or a repeat client—everyone gets the same level of dedication. We look at each relationship with a client as a lifelong relationship. We are trusted by families with their largest asset." Warren Buffett sought out Barbara Callan to sell his homes and, as the single most successful investor of the 20th century, he clearly knew the real deal when he saw it.

www.streetsofsanfrancisco.com

"WE ABSOLUTELY GO ABOVE AND BEYOND TO GET THE BEST TRANSACTION FOR OUR CLIENTS, WHETHER THEY ARE BUYING OR SELLING"

CALIFORNIA DREAMING

Kevin Aaronson—the realtor behind The Aaronson Group
—knows exactly what high-rolling clients are looking for
on one of the West Coast's most exclusive strips

The spectacular coastal stretch between Monarch Beach and Newport Beach in Orange County, California is home to an elite band of property owners who include Fortune 500 CEOs, top-level athletes, and Hollywood movie stars. Golf fanatics flock to the area's world-class Pelican Hill resort. Bette Midler's Oscar-nominated *Beaches* was filmed there, and the area has always attracted celebrities—from John Wayne to Nicolas Cage to Kobe Bryant—for decades.

Since 1998, Kevin Aaronson has found more than a few of them their dream home. Kevin heads up The Aaronson Group, one of the area's most successful realtor businesses, selling luxury properties between $3 million and $30 million to a discerning clientele. "I've spent a lot of time and energy studying the market here," says Kevin. "In this small stretch of highly sought-after coastal real estate, we have stunning properties from areas such as Newport Beach, Corona del Mar, Newport Coast, and Laguna Beach. Even though all are comparable in value, each location features its own sense of community, culture, and lifestyle."

A personal relationship
It's this keen knowledge of Orange County's luxury market that's helped The Aaronson Group achieve more than $100 million in sales volume over the last few years alone.

"One of my more memorable sales was to clients from the East Coast, who were looking for a vacation home," says Kevin. "After getting to know each other, and finding out their specific needs and preferences, I found a property for them

in Crystal Cove—a community in Newport Coast. The previous owner had spent around $1.5 million on the exterior alone, which boasted impressive views of the ocean and Catalina Island. As golfers, the clients also fell in love with the house's close proximity to Pelican Hill golf course, which is renowned as one of the best in the world. I believe that developing a close relationship with clients is crucial in order to find their dream property."

However, while purchasing at this level is very exclusive, Kevin says that one mantra of

home buying still applies. "It doesn't matter if it is a $300,000 home or a $30 million home, you should never compromise on location," he says. "You can always make structural changes or plant trees to increase privacy for the most part, but you can't change your location or view."

So whether it's a neighborhood with A-list exclusivity or a home with a multi-million dollar sea view, The Aaronson Group provides the perfect piece of paradise every time.
www.previewochomes.com

Chapter 8
CONCIERGE

THE BREWHOUSE INN AND SUITES

www.brewhousesuites.com

Originally the Pabst Brewery, this superb 90-suite Victorian-meets-the-21st-century-style hotel, pub, and grill is inspired throughout by its brewing past.
Milwaukee, WI

THE OYSTER POINT HOTEL

www.theoysterpointhotel.com

On the banks of the Navesink River, this elegant hotel offers a selection of stylish rooms and suites, along with its own marina and waterfront dining.
Red Bank, NJ

MERITAGE MEADOWS INN

www.meritagemeadows.com

Set in 14 acres of meadows and woodlands, this idyllic escape offers creature comforts, wine tastings, and easy access to the bright lights of Seattle.
Redmond, WA

ANTRIM 1844 COUNTRY HOUSE HOTEL

www.antrim1844.com

This strikingly beautiful country house hotel comprises an elegant, white-columned mansion along with 10 stylishly presented outbuildings that offer a range of luxury accommodation. Set amid a 450-acre estate and built in its namesake year, Antrim 1844 now includes a fine-dining restaurant, an all-weather tennis court and croquet pitch, a nature trail, and an expansive wine cellar. Also home to a glass-enclosed pavilion and rose garden, the hotel is the ideal setting for a lavish wedding, indulgent break, or upscale corporate get-together.
Taneytown, MD

HYATT REGENCY TAMAYA

www.tamaya.hyatt.com

Located in a culturally rich region at the foot of the Sandia Mountains, this lavish resort and spa offers world-class pampering services and golf facilities.
Santa Ana Pueblo, NM

THE DUKE MANSION

www.dukemansion.org

Built in 1915 and listed on the National Register of Historic Places, this grand, 20-roomed inn blends Southern charm with high-end luxury.
Charlotte, NC

THE CHRYSALIS INN & SPA

www.thechrysalisinn.com

With each of its rooms overlooking the stunning Pacific Northwest seascape, this sophisticated inn features a spa, restaurant, bar, and luxury suites.
Bellingham, WA

BONNEVILLE HOT SPRINGS RESORT AND SPA

www.bonnevilleresort.com

Renowned for its healing mineral waters, the town of North Bonneville is a must for those seeking relaxation and rejuvenation, as exemplified by this ultimate health haven. The resort's restaurant makes excellent use of the Pacific Northwest's delicious local produce in a mouthwatering menu that is accompanied by a world-class wine list. Guests can also enjoy the resort's newly re-sculpted links-style golf course, pool, indoor and outdoor hot tubs, dry sauna, and spa, which offers an extensive range of well-being and salon services.
North Bonneville, WA

WHITESTONE COUNTRY INN

www.whitestoneinn.com

With its own farmhouse, southern lodgings and chapel, this charming, 600-acre lakeside getaway offers refined country living and outdoor pursuits.
Kingston, TN

DONNA'S PREMIER LODGING

www.donnasofberlin.com

Set in the heart of Ohio's Amish country, Donna's offers luxury log cabins, bridal suites, and cosy chalets for an unforgettable romantic getaway.
Berlin, OH

FOUR SEASONS RESORT RANCHO ENCANTADO SANTA FE

www.fourseasons.com/santafe

Set in the Sangre de Cristo foothills, this resort offers 65 rooms and suites, an award-winning spa, and the Terra restaurant with locally inspired fare.
Santa Fe, NM

LA COQUILLADE

www.coquillade.fr

Located in the Luberon region of Provence, this opulent hotel offers relaxation, leisure activities, and a menu created by a Michelin-starred chef.
Gargas, France

ATHOLL PALACE HOTEL

www.athollpalace.com

Live out your baronial fantasies at this stunning Victorian hotel. Incredible views and highland hospitality ensure a fabulous stay.
Pitlochry, Perthshire, Scotland

SEAVIEW HOUSE HOTEL

www.seaviewhousehotel.com

Situated in an area famed for its tranquility, this delightful four-star country house hotel overlooks Bantry Bay and provides a host of leisure pursuits.
Ballylickey, Co. Cork, Ireland

INDEX

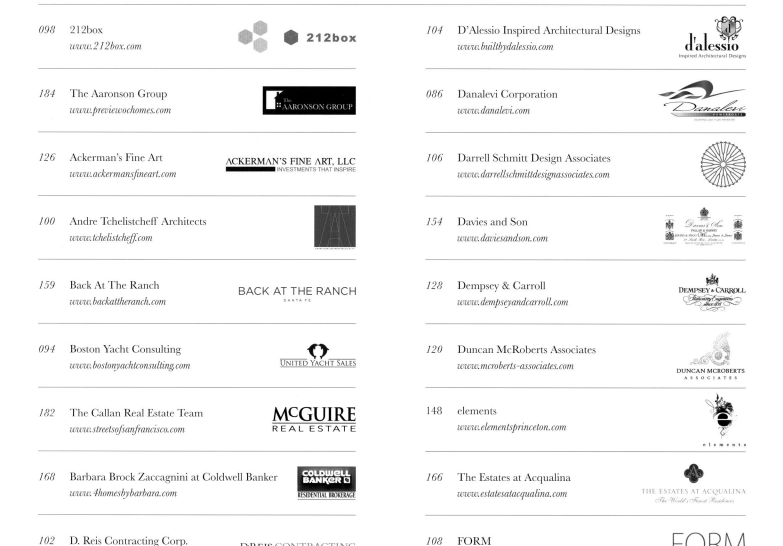